TO OZ AND BACK

Larry Garner

Editor: Kathy Lowe

Cover design: Roger Huddle

Cover photography: Jeremy Virag

A CIP catalogue record for this book is available from the British Library.

Published by Bramley Press

www.bramleypress.co.uk/ozandback

ISBN 978-0-9571325-3-5

For Cathy

Acknowledgements

A big thank you to the people who have helped and encouraged me with this book, especially my wife Cathy, my daughters Carolyn and Cori, Dave Mason, and everyone who worked at Sepon between 2003 and 2010— you know who you are.

Contents

1

'Land of opportunity'

Sitting with the lads in the pub, scanning the football results, gossip and half-truths in the Sunday paper, I spotted an advert headed 'Australia, Land of Opportunity.' The Australian immigration scheme designed to persuade people from the UK to move Down Under was stepping up its publicity drive. In 1973 you could jump on a plane or ship and be transported half way around the world for just £10.

The advert made me think about the recent past, and my future. I'd left school in 1967 only to spend the next 12 months wondering if I'd done the right thing. I'd become an apprentice fitter and turner, a job I hated, and though I lived for football at the weekends, the team I was playing for mirrored my life at that time—inexperienced, limp and spiritless. I had no money, no love life and my chosen profession seemed a dead end.

During the course of that year, having met up again with some old mates from school, I discovered they shared many of my thoughts and fears. At the age of 17 we'd been so quick to turn our backs on school and everything it stood for, forgetting that our friendship with each other had been the most important thing there.

We started to spend more time together, meeting for a drink on Wednesday nights, and these thoroughly enjoyable evenings in the pub pulled me through a particularly dark period. All of us were football mad and had played for the school team. In fact our last season had been the school's most successful ever. So one night after a few beers, someone's suggestion that we try to form an Old Boys' squad was met with a resounding yes. We re-formed in time for the start of the 1968-69 season and were soon going from strength to strength.

Now, a few seasons later here we were, sitting in the Canon with another season drawing to a close, complaining bitterly that our dream of an unbeaten season had been whisked away from us by a frozen pitch and short-sighted referee. I looked out of the window as I waited for my drinks. A light dust of snow covered the cars in the car park outside, while inside a fire in the hearth warmed the bar and the atmosphere.

I would soon be 21 and I badly needed a change—we all did. 'Here we are lads,' I announced, '"Australia, Land of Opportunity" and it'll only cost us 10 quid to get there.'

'You fancy that, do you?' asked Rob Allen, a lad I'd known since our first day of school.

'I do Rob. I finish me time in May: we could be on Bondi Beach in July.

'It's winter there in July,' someone said.

'Alright then we could be playing football on Bondi in July.' I wasn't knocked over by their enthusiasm, but it was a start and that Sunday evening I filled in the application form that started the ball rolling.

There were six of us who would be completing our respective apprenticeships in the next few months, all very useful young men Australia needed. We lived in the town of

Borehamwood, the Wood as we called it, just 13 miles from the centre of London. From my bedroom window you could see cows—smell them too if the wind was blowing in the right direction. Yet jump on the train and I could be in London St Pancras station in 16 minutes, or at work in under an hour. I guess we had the best of both worlds but after 20 years none of it had any appeal anymore.

I had little confidence that all six of us would go to Australia. Rob seemed to have the world by the balls already. Women loved him and men wanted to be like him as the saying goes, and it seemed whatever he turned his hand to he found the knack of doing it properly. He was training as a printer but had other plans. Although he'd given me a tentative nod when I suggested Australia, I knew he wouldn't be there playing football with us on Bondi Beach.

Lenny Phillips was the other in the group who I'd known since our first day of school. He was a fitter and turner just like me, and like me he wanted more than was on offer. Of the six of us he was the one I was certain would come with me.

John, another printer, and still working at the place where he did his apprenticeship, seemed already in a rut and in need of a jolt to get him out of it. He was a very good footballer and a chick magnet, always useful to have around as Lenny and I picked up the crumbs.

Joe was in IT long before it meant anything to most people. Another one the girls liked and almost as doubtful as Rob, he might surprise me, I thought. In the football team he was our worst player, more enthusiasm than skill. He could run all day—usually because his first touch was so bad he had to!

Frank, also a printer, seemed to have the skills that make a professional footballer, except he played brilliantly one week and couldn't get into the game the next. He might just opt for Australia if Joe and the others decided to go too.

A week later I received a thick envelope in the mail with six application forms to emigrate to Australia and as I handed them out on the Wednesday night I received my first knock back. Rob smiled. 'No, I'm sorry Lol, I'll never leave here, not even for a couple of years. Do you really think that you will?'

'It all starts with the first step Rob,' I tried to explain. But I'd known before I even sent off for the forms that he wouldn't be with us on Bondi. The others all filled out their applications for me to send with mine to Australia House in central London.

That football season, my last with Brookside as it turned out, was possibly our best ever. We finished top of our division, winning our League Cup by beating a team two divisions above us 7-0 in the Cup Final. I remember training harder than anyone towards the end of that season, running through the damp streets in the rain. England was cold and wet and I was tired of both.

2

All change

Australia had never been top of my list of countries to visit, let alone live in. Yet here I was one August day in 1973 about to catch the four-thirty flight from London Heathrow to Perth in search of a better life Down Under. I was 21, leaving on my own, and utterly terrified.

Everyone gathered in the Shooting Star to see me off. I'd lived in Boreham Wood for most of my life and had known many of the people present for as long as I could remember. As I circulated saying my goodbyes, many told me they wished they were going with me. I wished they were too.

Musky, a bloke I served my apprenticeship with, had managed to get away from work for an hour. Shaking my hand with tears in his eyes he asked, 'Do you reckon you'll ever return to the Wood?' I shrugged my shoulders. 'Return to the Wood? I haven't left yet.'

I was chatting to Mark Readings, an old school mate, when my dad tapped me on the shoulder. 'Time to go son.' Very reluctantly I squeezed myself out of the pub, trying hard to control my emotions. I failed miserably as the thought of leaving washed over me.

In the small convoy that left the Shooting Star for the airport, I travelled with my dad, my youngest sister Debs and my girlfriend Elaine. A few others included Rob and a couple of the lads from the football club in Len's car and my other sister Dene and future brother-in-law travelling in their car, with a few strays.

We made the airport in time for a final a drink in the bar where I remember I had the biggest lump in my throat and the beer tasted like vinegar. It would have been so easy to change my mind about going, return with them to the Star, and carry on in my rut. Instead I headed for the departure gate and, giving my Dad and Elaine a hug, quickly passed the point of no return.

Looking back I have never regretted the decision. It was without doubt the hardest—and best—thing I ever did.

3

Going it alone

The flight to Perth took forever, thirty eight hours. Thirty eight hours! Plenty of time to think about those I was leaving behind ....

My dad had grown concerned when I told him of my desire to emigrate. He hadn't tried to put me off the idea, but hadn't encouraged me either. I don't think he ever saw me as a traveller—just hoped that it was another phase I was going through. Only when he saw that I was talking with a passion and some excitement about leaving, did he begin to accept that his only son might be going to the other side of the world. I had always been close to him. He raised me and my two sisters on a North London council estate after our mother walked out. (I came home from school one day to find she'd gone and I haven't seen her since.)

I wanted my dad to understand that Australia offered something I felt England could never offer me: an encouraging future. One night, after we had been out for a drink together, he showed he had come to terms with losing me and wished me all the best. This was the green light I needed from him to continue guilt-free.

I never thought I'd be going alone though. I had my mates and my girlfriend Elaine. God, I loved Elaine. She was everything I wanted in a woman. We had been together for about two years in a relationship that carried me through my poverty stricken days as an apprentice. She lived in Liverpool, a two hundred mile trip up the motorway, and we had talked about moving in together when I finished my training. Strangely enough the plan to emigrate hadn't up to that point involved Elaine: I hadn't even told her.

At the end of the football season we enjoyed a wonderful weekend in the Lake District as Mr and Mrs Smith, and it was there that I first raised my plans to emigrate. At first Elaine was lukewarm about the idea, as I had expected, but as the miserable spring rolled into an even more miserable summer, my enthusiasm to leave became infectious. Although I had actually decided to go whether Elaine wanted to or not, I was elated when she phoned one evening to tell me she had applied to emigrate too.

My elation was short-lived. Within days of hearing that Elaine had applied, my mates Frankie and Joe both bailed out together. I tried to sweet talk them, but when it comes to emigrating to the other side of the world, you either want to go or you don't. So that left me, John, Lenny and possibly Elaine.

I had finished my apprenticeship at the end of May after five years, and had moved up to Liverpool where I lived with Elaine in her parents' home. It was far from ideal but we were together, and I enjoyed the short time we spent there in her tiny room.

I got a job driving a truck, as it paid more than I could earn in my trade as a fitter. I drove mostly local runs up and down the East Lancs Road, filling in until either something better came along or until Australia materialised. Having recently seen a documentary about the mining boom in Australia I knew I would be paid what I was worth over there and that made me more determined than ever to go. I just hoped they would accept Elaine's application.

Early in June the letter with our tickets, paperwork and departure dates arrived. With our departure scheduled for July 17, Elaine and I drove down to London on the first weekend in June to meet Lenny and John who had also received their tickets. At last things were really starting to happen.

Rod Stewart was playing at Liverpool's Anfield Stadium a week before we were scheduled to leave, and Lenny and most of the other lads were coming up to see me and go to the concert. Before the concert, however, something happened that changed everything. I was at work, just about ready to drive out of the depot, when I received a phone call from Elaine to say her father had been involved in an accident. Jack had been knocked off his bike by a bus on Scotty Road and had died on the spot. He was 54.

Elaine and her mother Alice were inconsolable. I got in touch with the Australian Consulate in London who were very understanding, and told me to contact them for another date as soon as we were ready.

The evening before the Rod Stewart concert the lads told me that they weren't coming to the concert. I thought it was out of respect for Elaine's Dad and thanked them. Then Lenny phoned me.

'Lol, it's Len. Listen, I'm not coming.'

'Yeah I know. Rob called earlier. Elaine and I aren't going to the concert either as it's too soon after the funeral.'

'No you don't understand ... I'm not coming to Australia.'

'Why?' There was a long silence. It seemed a simple question, but one Lenny had trouble answering.

'I've never wanted to go Lol. I just didn't think it would come this far. I'm sorry mate. There's nothing more to say except that John wants me to tell you that he isn't going either.'

'To the concert or Australia?'

'Both!'

I put the phone down. I couldn't believe Lenny wasn't coming. In a way I was glad John had dropped out because if it had been just him and me we probably would have split as soon as we got there. But Len ... I was so disappointed. I looked out of Elaine's bedroom window across the grey slate-tiled roofs. Then I shrugged. 'Fuck it!' I said to myself, 'I'm not staying here.' Elaine and I were still going and the two of us could start a new life in Australia together. If anything I liked the idea even more.

As summer arrived I started to broach the delicate subject of Australia with Elaine again.

'I can't leave me mum like this,' she told me in no uncertain terms. Time slipped by, July drifted into August and then one Sunday evening everything became crystal clear. Elaine and I returned from a walk in the local park to find a tearful Alice sitting at the kitchen table.

'Do you remember when there were six of us around this table, hardly room to move? I won't have that problem anymore, will I?' Alice said through a twisted smile.

It was then that I knew Elaine and I wouldn't be going to Australia together.

'I can't leave her like this.' Elaine told me again.

'I know, but I can't stay either.'

Elaine and I never really broke up; we simply grew apart. The passing years and thousands of miles would do that.

4
Real Perth

On the flight to Australia we stopped in Zurich, Beirut, Bombay and Singapore, arriving in Perth late Saturday night totally exhausted. In those days the on-board entertainment consisted of one movie and half a dozen songs relayed to the hapless economy passenger through a blue tube with really abrasive ear pieces. Whenever I hear *Gypsies, Tramps and Thieves* by Cher I'm transported right back to that weekend, painful for so many emotional and physical reasons, but with those earplugs the most painful memory of all.

I passed through customs, collected my case and toolbox, and then slowly filed out into the arrivals hall feeling very tired, very lost and terribly lonely.

'All the single immigrants over here please,' said a grey haired guy with a handwritten banner reading 'Single Poms'. 'I guess that's me,' I said to myself.

'Single immigrants over here please,' he repeated.

A woman was calling for families. I approached the bloke looking for the singles.

'Laurence Garner,' I told him, offering my hand.

'Fred Davis,' he smiled as he ticked off my name from a short list. 'Hang on here son; there are a couple of others.' He wore a familiar gold and black Wolves football shirt, which for some reason made me feel a little less lost.

Slowly after a few minutes the crowd thinned leaving three of us, a bit beaten around the edges, standing around Fred. We were the obviously the single immigrants.

Fred ushered us outside into the car park where a minibus waited.

'Any of you lads play football?' he asked as we loaded our gear into a box trailer behind the bus.

'I do,' I told him.

'Any good?'

'I'm brilliant, that why I'm here.' I realised this was the first time I'd spoken in over a day. My sarcasm wasn't lost on anyone and it broke the ice. We started talking as we drove out of the airport on the way to our hostel.

'Do you fancy a game tomorrow?' Fred asked as he shifted through the gears. I looked at my watch to find it was just after midnight.

'What time?' I asked.

'Eleven o'clock.'

'Yeah alright, I'll have some of that.'

Fred took us to the hostel, booking us in and promising to pick me up at ten the following day. My two new mates and I were now wide awake so, having spotted Coke and ice machines in the lobby, we brought out our bottles of duty free, found some glasses for a toast and wished each other all the best in our new country.

We hadn't been to bed and had managed to drain three bottles of Scotch between us by the time Fred arrived the next morning. It was hardly the best preparation for a game of football I've ever had, but I was ready for my first game in Australia. Fred was still wearing the Wolves shirt and as we drove to the game, I found out that he was not only from Wolverhampton but had actually played for Wolves in the

1950s. I liked him immediately, not because he was an ex-pro but because he was extremely charismatic, easy to talk to and a compulsive liar.

Our opposition was a team that called themselves Real Perth. They looked professional in their replica Real Madrid strip, but fortunately for us the kit was the only thing about them that resembled the Spanish masters. As I came off after our 5-0 win I thought I'd given a good account of myself.

'You've played before,' was all Fred said as I walked into the dressing room, but I understood the back-handed compliment.

It was a little after one when I came out of the changing room. The early morning drizzle had blown away, the sun was out, and it had all the makings of being a very pleasant afternoon.

'Where are you going now?' asked one of the lads, whose name I still hadn't grasped.

'I don't know', I honestly replied, 'I'm knackered.' I hadn't slept for about three days.

'Come along with me mate, we're off to Chris's place.'

Twenty minutes later I was sitting under a tree with a beer in one hand, a sausage sandwich in the other, and holding two conversations at once. It felt like I'd never ever been anywhere else.

5

Jobs for the boys

I woke up on Monday morning with a purpose. The Saturday edition of the *West Australian* had a number of promising adverts, so I was setting off to fill out applications for employment and see a bit of Perth at the same time. Alan and Lindsay, the two lads I arrived with were as keen as I was to get started and came into town with me.

We were being put up in the Greylands hostel, which was comfortable, clean but temporary. Although we'd been told we could live there for two weeks before being charged rent, I had plans to be gone long before then. We caught the bus into town and I headed to the offices of the mining companies on Adelaide Terrace.

We separated at the Wentworth Hotel, agreeing to meet there when we'd finished. A few minutes later I was filling out applications in the first mining company office, and having my papers photocopied. After a half an hour I was told that someone would contact me in a couple of days, and I left the building feeling optimistic. Just across the road I found the offices of a second mining company where I spent well over an hour, had an interview and was told that subject to a satisfactory medical examination I had a job! A date for the medical was set, and I almost floated back to the Wentworth where Alan and Lindsay were waiting for me.

'How did it go?' I asked, barely able to contain myself.

'Good,' replied Alan. 'I've dropped off a few CVs and everyone I spoke to asked me when I could start.'

Alan was an electrician. I told him that they were looking for 'sparkies' where I had been, but he wasn't keen to go to the bush just yet, preferring to experience Perth first.

'How about you Linds?' I asked.

'Same. I could even get a job here in the hotel.'

Lindsay, who was a chef, had learned that the manager of the Wentworth desperately needed a good chef on his staff and was offering accommodation with the job. All in all the three of us had spent a very successful morning.

We had lunch at the Wentworth before returning to the hostel, where we found someone waiting for us in the lobby.

'Hello, are you the new arrivals?' he asked.

'Yeah,' said Alan. 'We arrived on Saturday night.'

'Dave Reynolds,' he said and handed us a card each. 'I'm from the showroom over the road on the Stirling Highway.'

I had noticed the yard as we arrived over the weekend, and was thinking about having a look. As we had waited for a bus that morning the three of us had briefly discussed our need for a car, but I soon realised that those in this particular yard—including a very attractive Valiant Charger that had caught my eye—were way out of my range.

I arrived in Australia with just $260 and after being in the country 48 hours I now had $250 to last me until whenever pay day would be.

Slippery Dave, as we called him, took us across to his yard. While Alan and Lindsay were a bit better off than me, and in the market for a car, they weren't going to buy the first one they saw. Slippery turned his attention to me.

'So you like the Charger do you?'

'Yes, it's a good looking car but out of my league.'

'Not in this country. No deposit, nothing down, you could drive it away tomorrow.'

I smiled. 'I don't think so Dave.' Still, a seed had been sown.

6

Temptation on wheels

My medical, scheduled for the following Wednesday afternoon, turned out to be a formality and I sailed through the examination. I was fit, I knew that.

I had trained the previous night with Fred's teams and on the way back to the hostel I walked past the car yard again. The Charger gleamed under the lights, an attractive dark blue motor with chrome mags. It was doing 100 miles an hour just sitting there. Maybe I could afford it.

Slippery Dave didn't give up easily, sensing perhaps that he might have a bit of bait with the Charger. I took it for a test drive on the anniversary of our first week in Australia. Impressed, I asked how much it would cost, say, over five years with no deposit, only to learn that the drive-away price was over $8,000 and change.

I laughed. 'Until I get a job I haven't even got the change.'

'I've told you, you don't need money in this country.'

'I haven't even got a job yet Dave,' I repeated.

To me $5,000 was a king's ransom so $8,000 was

completely out of the question ... or was it?

That weekend Lindsay started work at the Wentworth, so Alan and I helped him move from the hostel before heading into town that evening to a couple of pubs and a club. Our night out wasn't exactly a great success. Alan, I decided, was a bit of baggage I needed to lose: we were different, very different. With Lindsay there was a balance, yet I knew that when we finally went our separate ways I wouldn't be looking for Alan's company.

I played a good game of football again on the Sunday, scoring another goal in the 5-0 massacre of a team from Fremantle. It turned out to be my last game for the team. I enjoyed the barbecue that followed and thought I might enjoy living in Perth but I was on a mission, with no intention of repeating what I had been doing in England. Having been poor all my life I needed to become a miner and earn some money. This meant going where the mines were. You never find gold on a city street, or iron ore for that matter.

When Fred dropped me back at the hostel I told him of my plans and he seemed genuinely disappointed that he was losing his new centre half.

'Good luck son,' he said shaking my hand, 'you'll do alright.'

I thanked him for all he had done for me and as he drove off I walked across to the yard to inspect the Charger for the umpteenth time. It was Sunday evening and no one should have been around, but slippery Dave was watching from the hostel. He knew that car had my name on it.

'Take it for a spin,' he said, startling me.

'Don't you have a day off?'

'Sunday afternoon is probably my busiest time of the week.'

I capitulated and took the Charger for another drive. By eight o'clock that night I'd signed on the dotted line.

The following morning I received the letter of offer from Mt Newman Mining. In those days you knew the result of an interview by the size of the envelope. A small envelope contained a single piece of paper telling you 'thanks, but no thanks'. A big envelope contained a contract, brochures and reams of information. I liked the big envelopes.

After Alan and I went into town to meet Lindsay at the Wentworth, I stopped at MNM's office to sign the contract. I explained I wouldn't need the air ticket they were offering me as I'd be driving to Port Hedland.

I said goodbye to Alan and Lindsay over lunch, before making my way back to the hostel. Having picked up the car from Slippery Dave, I parked outside my room in the hostel, loaded my worldly possessions and my toolbox into the boot, and was heading out of Perth by three o'clock.

7

Perth to Port Hedland

I reached Geraldton in just under four hours. Many people had advised me not to drive after dark in Australia because of kangaroos. (Over the years since then I have driven all over Australia and seen the wreckage that a kangaroo or even a scrub turkey in the road can cause.) So I was relieved to arrive in Geraldton just as it was getting dark. Thirsty and tired, I spotted a pub, sat at the bar and immediately struck up a conversation with a fella next to me.

'Where you headed?' he asked. He was obviously a local and I obviously wasn't.

'Port Hedland.'

'Got a bit of a drive in front of you then.'

'How far?'

'About 1200 klicks. It's bitumen as far as Roebourne and dirt the rest of the way. This time of year the rivers aren't too high, so getting through won't be a problem.'

This was going to be quite the adventure. I bought my new mate a drink and ordered a counter tea. We talked for another half hour.

'Where're you staying?' he asked me.

'I'll probably stay here.'

'Come with me,' he said. 'I've got a few spare beds at the station where you can camp if you like.' I'd met the local fire chief, and I spent that night in the Geraldton fire station.

There were no callouts that night, so I slept uninterrupted, even waking in the morning to a fresh cooked breakfast. I then said goodbye to the Fire Chief and continued up the West Coast. The very uneventful 500 kilometre journey from Geraldton to Carnarvon took me five hours. I then had lunch, fuelled up and got back on the road just after twelve thirty.

North of Carnarvon my route was flat and straight, handled comfortably by the Charger at 150 kilometres an hour. I was the only person on the road and I waved as an occasional car passed me in the opposite direction.

The terrain changed to desert—a new experience for me—and I stopped and got out for a walk. It was about three o'clock and boy was it hot. (I'm going to be working in this heat I thought, so I'd better get used to it.) But it was the wonderful silence that really struck me. I thought briefly about home and how far away that seemed now.

At high speed the car was really sucking down the petrol so I drove for the rest of the day doing about 90 kph until I ran out of daylight. About 30 kilometres from Roebourne I saw my first ever kangaroo and stopped for the night.

Camped beside the road, I ate a few things I'd bought in Carnarvon, wishing I had something hot to drink. With no light, and no city glare, there's nothing to prevent you seeing all the stars and I lay on the bonnet of the car with my feet on the roof looking up at the heavens. What a night! I thought of Dad and Elaine, wondering if they were thinking of me. When it finally became too cold to sit outside, I climbed into the back seat of the car and tried to rest. It was far from comfortable and I slept poorly.

I was on my way again at dawn, stopping only to refuel

in Roebourne and grab a much-needed breakfast before tackling the last leg of my journey.

Just after Roebourne the road turned to dirt or gravel and as the car wasn't designed for off-road driving, I took my time. A river crossing, where I feared the Charger would be, quite literally, out of its depth, presented a potential problem so I first walked across to check the river bed before easing the car through.

Whim Creek was a sight for sore eyes and totally unexpected. I came around a bend to find a pub in the wilderness. Although it was still only mid-morning I felt I'd already been travelling for ages so couldn't wait to get to the bar. I was amused to find a camel drinking beer in there, so I bought him one.

I got to the Sherlock river about midday—serious, fast-flowing waters entirely different from the first creek I'd crossed. On the opposite bank a couple of seasoned four-wheel drivers had pulled up to discuss the best course of action. A lot of white water suggested the river wasn't in fact too deep, so I decided to go ahead, watched by the small crowd on the far bank as I dipped and lurched through the water. Apart from a tiny stretch where the water started to climb up the door and an anxious moment when one of the front wheels sank into a hole and the water lapped over the bonnet, it was a walk in the park.

As I climbed the far bank I was waved down by one of the Land Rover drivers.

'You've obviously done that before. Any advice?'

'Just keep her in low range and let her find her own way,' I said, trying to sound as if I did this every day. Low range! If they only knew the truth.

I continued on my way wondering how much further I had to go, when the road suddenly changed back to bitumen, and I finally found myself on the outskirts of Port Hedland Shire.

The screen house was visible in the distance—the iron

ore processing plant which, although I didn't know it then, would be my home for the next 12 months. It was another hour's drive before I hit the outskirts of town. I drove through the suburbs until I eventually pulled into the car park at Nelson Point. Clutching my letter of introduction I reported to the gatehouse, and after a few minutes I was shown to a temporary room. As it was Sunday with no-one here to officially welcome me, I was allowed to take my car in and drop off my case and toolbox.

Left to my own devices I then turned on the air conditioner and slumped onto the bed. I'd made it. These days the road from Perth to Port Hedland is bitumen all the way and offers no excitement at all. When I did it, I felt I had learned a bit about myself—that I had achieved something. Yeah, I was very pleased with myself.

8

Becoming Larry

When I was a kid I studied *The Atlas of the World,* a colourful junior version that was my first book. From a young age I was interested in the world and my place in it, literally. Even before I went to school I could name the major rivers of the world and half of its capital cities.

The way I used to pore over the atlas until it was falling apart so impressed my dad that he bought me a *Times Atlas*, a massive book with the finest of details I never tired of reading. I'd pick a page and imagine myself being there: how would I get from Kampala to Mombasa, I'd ask myself, or Calgary to Vancouver? It was something I never wearied of, and something I still do today.

As I got older, I wrote down a list of places I wanted to visit, such as Kavieng, in New Ireland and Manado in Selawesi. I also pencilled in Port Hedland, isolated on the North West coast of Australia and seemingly miles from absolutely anywhere. Unfortunately it was not quite the romantic location I imagined.

My first day began with a mandatory 15 minute

induction, followed by a walk across the compound to the screen house I'd heard about, where the iron ore is processed. I had hoped I might find my way into the loco shed or machine shop, but everyone in the trade had done time in the screen house and I was not going to be an exception.

When a bloke I'd met at the hostel in Perth had heard I was off to the iron ore mines in the North West, he'd taken me shopping at an army surplus store for what he thought would be the appropriate clothing—three khaki army shirts and some shorts resembling Bombay bloomers. Now on my first day in the screen house office I sat looking every bit like an extra from *It Ain't Half Hot Mum,* the 1970s TV comedy series set in the jungles of Burma. For an hour I sat there, the object of much scrutiny from various members of staff, while Gordon, the company clerk, tried to decide what to do with me.

'Who is he?' I heard someone whisper. Heads shook and I was left alone for a few more minutes drinking coffee while Gordon sifted through some more papers. He was convinced I was senior management because no one dressed like me worked in the screen house.

'Are you Laurence Garner?' he eventually asked.

'Yeah,' I nodded, feeling a little relieved.

Happy his dilemma had finally been sorted, Gordon laughed. 'I thought you were someone, y'know someone a bit more ... er ... important,' he stumbled.

'I'm sorry,' I apologised, not really sure what I was apologising for. Gordon picked up the tannoy to call for someone and about five minutes later a bloke came in to the office who looked like an Adonis.

'Denny this is Laurence.' As we shook hands I noted that Den, dressed in just a pair of shorts and covered in sweat, stood nearly six feet tall. He had broad shoulders and thick arms. The iron ore dust that stuck to him gave him a dark complexion, making his white teeth shine even whiter when he smiled.

'Come with me kid,' Den said in his strong Geordie

accent. He was from Newcastle, England, and I liked him immediately. He took me up to the screen floor where 22 screens, like big sieves, were separating the oversized chunks of ore from the finer stuff. The huge pan feeders that deposited ore onto the screens vibrated noisily, creating clouds of fine dust that hung in the air like talcum powder and got into everything.

I was introduced to Denny's crew.

'Jimmy, Laurence.'

'Frank, Laurence.'

'Bernie, Laurence.'

'Fuck me Laurence, what else do they call you?' Den asked.

Jimmy chimed in, 'Larry. They call someone who's Laurence, Larry don't they?'

From that moment on I became Larry.

At smoko we all trooped into the smoko hut, sat down, and took a good look at one another.

'Well first thing, this shirt needs a bit of tailoring,' someone suggested. A knife was produced and in a couple of minutes the sleeves were removed from the shirt. I also found myself on the receiving end of a bit of verbal. I'm English from London, the capital of the world, but my new crew who were nearly all sweaty socks didn't share my beliefs. Neither did Denny the Geordie, Dermot from Dublin, nor Bernie from New Plymouth, New Zealand. I was going to have to prove myself to everyone, especially Jimmy, because Denny told me I was going to be working with him.

'Right, let's get something straight right from the start,' Jimmy told me. 'You're my fitter and I'm not your bleedin' TA (trades assistant). Got it?'

I got it. Jimmy was five feet five inches and weighed about 100 pounds. I've seen more fat on a chip, but he looked fierce and as tenacious as a Jack Russell terrier so I saw no point in upsetting the wee man.

Over time, my first instinct proved right on the money.

While I can handle myself, Jimmy was one of those lads who simply enjoyed fighting and never lost. Even if he lost the initial confrontation, he wouldn't sleep until he got even.

We returned to the screen Jimmy had been working on. Each screen deck has five woven wire mats and I went into the bottom deck to learn how to install them. There was a knack to it, especially where room was kind of tight. I soon learned that you didn't need a shirt, a hard hat or glasses— just the right attitude.

At the end of the job I had to climb into the chute under the screen to ensure that nothing had fallen through that would foul further down the plant. I then had to remove a heavy plate above the live conveyor that needed all my strength to open. Dust fell like a heavy black curtain, blinding and nearly suffocating me, and I emerged looking like the blob from the black lagoon.

At the end of the first day it seemed I had passed the test and been accepted by this unusual but likeable crew. As I walked back to my room in their company, I felt different from the bloke who had gone to the induction that morning. I certainly looked different.

A shower never felt better and the beer that followed tasted like nectar, especially the first one. A good evening meal and a bit of TV brought my first day to a close.

I met my room-mate Jim Sullivan, a Yank from Washington State who seemed slightly out of place. I was pleased to be sharing with a bloke who didn't drink. I had heard stories about drunken room mates who would be abusive or who, in their drunken stupor, would accidentally use the closet at the end of the bed as a toilet. Jim liked a good chat, but I remember on the first night I could hardly keep my eyes open and fell asleep before he could start.

9

Sticky situations

The screen house loomed over the town, dominating the skyline from every direction. When the trains came in from Mount Newman, 400 kilometres inland, the iron ore in the trucks was emptied at the car dumper onto conveyors. These took the ore up to the top of the screen house where it was fed onto vibrating screens that worked like giant sieves sorting the ore into three sizes. Oversized ore was sent to the crusher to be reduced to about 30 mil: coarse ore was between 10 and 30 mil: and fine ore was anything under 10 mil.

After being sorted and processed in the screen house, the iron ore found its way out into the yard where it was stacked in massive stock piles ready to be reclaimed. Then it was loaded into giant cargo ships bound for Japan, where it was made into steel. Finally, the steel was turned into Toyotas and imported back into Australia a few months later.

The whole ore processing operation was performed in extremely hot and humid working conditions. While I was there the temperature rarely dropped below 35°C, and frequently rose to over 40°C. Marble Bar, the hottest place in

Australia, was just down the road. Humidity in the plant reached 90 per cent: water just ran out of the air conditioners: there was no ventilation and we breathed iron ore dust.

The shirts we wore to work were discarded as soon as we started. In those days before employers had to take account of duty-of-care requirements I wore just a pair of shorts, boots and socks. The rest of the kit supplied was definitely optional. These days the mining industry is saturated with petty little rules driven by insurance companies and put in place by foolish people who have never spent a day in places like the screen house.

Having served my time as a fitter and turner I found that the maintenance work in the screen house was basic at best.

'A shifter and a hammer are all you need,' Denny told me when he saw my toolbox. I'd spent five years and a lot of money putting that toolbox together, but I realised I'd have to buy a shifter, the common term used to describe an adjustable spanner. None of the jobs we had to tackle needed a great deal of know-how. Sometimes, about once a week if we were really good, we were given a conveyor inspection—a task which gave us the freedom of the plant, and something Jimmy thought was just too good to be true.

For most of the 12 months we were in Hedland, Jimmy and I became almost inseparable. He hailed from Glasgow, was a Rangers supporter and hated the English with a passion, though for some reason he hated me less passionately. I like to think he almost liked me, which was definitely a plus because I saw on too many occasions what Jimmy was capable of if you got on the wrong side of him. He could fight like 10 men, and I once saw him bite off someone's ear lobe long before the boxer Mike Tyson made it fashionable.

There were two hotels in town, the Esplanade and the Pier, blood baths at any time of day, both of them. The town drew a cosmopolitan and motley crew from every corner of the earth, most of whom found their way into one pub or the other.

Thursday Islanders who worked on the rail gangs liked a drink. The Serbs and Croats who were definitely not Yugoslavians were partial to a cold beer on a warm afternoon, as were the short-fused Glaswegians. Then there were the occasional arrogant Frogs, Aboriginals, Kiwis, Poms and even the odd, very odd, Aussie. (In my time there, white Australian males were poorly represented.)

At almost any tick of the clock a united nations could be found in the beer garden of either of the two pubs. Mix that with just about any drink under the sun and the perpetual heat, and you had a volatile little cocktail that attracted Jimmy like a compass to the north.

When our conveyor inspection took us right out to the end of the pier that gave one of the pubs its name, Jimmy would find his way into the beer garden through a hole in the fence. I would leave him there and pick him up on my way back but sometimes he'd be missing. On two occasions we had to go to police station after work to bail him out.

10

Ninety Mile Beach

W e worked six days a week. Unless there were shutdowns or breakdowns, we normally had Sundays off and spent them getting into trouble. Just north of Port Hedland is Ninety Mile Beach, a wonderful natural feature that exists in very few places in the world where the desert simply runs into the ocean. From the top of the dunes a dip in the sea looks so tempting—except that in the Indian Ocean, just off the beach, lives almost every deadly species of marine life.

This was explained to me one Sunday morning. Four of us had left Hedland the previous night with every intension of getting to Broome in time for a drink on Sunday. We had yet to come to terms with the size of Australia however, forgetting it was 470 kilometres to Broome. Having lost interest at about midnight 100 kilometres north of Hedland we decided to camp on the beach.

As we were cooking breakfast over an open fire, sucking on the ever present can of beer, I stripped off and ran into the sea quickly followed by the others. We emerged from the water to be greeted by the police. Spotting our fire from their patrol car the law wandered down to investigate and found four Poms skinny dipping.

'Morning,' I said as genially as I could.

'Do you know that what you are doing is illegal?'

'What, skinny dipping?' I asked.

'No,' the law said tiredly, 'having a fire on the beach.'

'Oh come on man we're miles from anywhere—what possible harm could we possibly be doing?' argued Adam McQueen, the Scot who was a new addition to our crew.

'I don't have to explain the law, I only have to uphold it,' came the stock answer.

'But skinny dipping's alright?' Jimmy wanted to know.

'Certainly, in fact we encourage Poms to swim here.'

'Why? You reckon the sharks might get us?'

'Sharks are the least of your problems,' sniggered the copper. 'Out there, even in a few of those pools, are some of the deadliest creatures on this earth.'

Obligingly he listed them starting with the box jelly fish, the world's most dangerous creature; stone fish, the most venomous and certainly the ugliest; and the lethal blue ringed octopus. 'But probably the most dangerous and numerous in this part of the coast,' he said, 'are the sea snakes, some of which are more venomous than any land snake.' All of these, he assured us, were just sitting out there waiting for a Pom to swim out and join them.

'Shouldn't be a problem for me then, should it?' said Jimmy looking smaller than ever, as he stood naked beside the big cop.

'How's that then?' the cop demanded to know.

'I'm no' a Pom and I can' ne swim!'

11

The Wild West

I stayed away from the temptation of the pubs most week nights, but one Tuesday evening I made a phone call from the post office. I was with Adam McQueen who had become my roommate after Jim Sullivan left, and who joined me when he knew I was heading into town.

I'd come to call Elaine on her birthday. I had been away for about six weeks and I still thought of her as my girlfriend. I spoke to her for 10 minutes at a cost of about 60 dollars and my money seemed to run out all too soon. Still, I thought it was worth every penny just to hear her voice.

Afterwards Adam and I headed for the Esplanade Hotel to play a game of pool, but my mind was elsewhere and after a couple of games we retired to the bar. I sat there watching two guys playing on the table we had just vacated. It wasn't particularly late, but we were bored so we drank up and were about to go when something happened.

In West Australia they have the black ball pocket rule whereby you nominate a pocket when you are down to the black ball. You win the game by putting the black ball in your chosen pocket and you lose if the black ball goes in any other pocket.

The two guys playing were Yugoslavs who we knew vaguely from the screen house. Steve, the first guy, had nominated the top left hand pocket but over-hit his shot so that the black ball rattled around the top of the pocket without going down. The second player, who I knew as Shariff, tried something far from safe, failed miserably, and the ball rolled over to the nominated pocket to line up the simplest of shots for Steve.

In the blink of an eye Shariff picked up the black ball and hurled it furiously at Steve, hitting him with a sickening crack. Steve collapsed on to the table and rolled on to the floor bleeding quite badly from a head wound. Adam and I ran over to try to assist him as Shariff scarpered.

The barman phoned the ambulance, and within minutes the police were questioning us as the ambulance wailed away into the distance. Steve never woke up and died early the next morning—just another unwanted statistic for the Esplanade Hotel. They found Shariff out in the desert a couple of days later almost dead himself from dehydration and thirst. Apparently he and Steve had bet 100 dollars on the pool game, about a week's wages. Hardly worth dying for.

12

Christmas Test Match

Christmas came—my first ever Christmas in Australia. I wanted to work in order to keep my mind off where I'd rather be, but as we weren't needed at the screen house we decided to go to Marble Bar and spend Christmas in Australia's hottest spot. It was 47°C that day! And we played cricket!

After a two hour drive from Hedland on a dusty road, we reached Marble Bar just before mid-day. Brad, the only Aussie in our group, owned an old EH Holden station wagon with a dodgy radiator that overheated frequently. The car desperately needed a service, but despite a couple of unscheduled stops, we arrived in time for the lunchtime drinking session.

We booked into the Iron Clad Hotel where we met about a dozen lads from Goldsworthy who had decided to spend the day the same way as us. We checked each other out before having a few beers together, and before we knew it we were organising our own Test Match—England v Australia. Asking around the bar if anyone was interested in playing, we found a few takers and at about two o'clock in the heat of the day (after the pub had closed of course) England went in to bat.

No fewer than seven Scots were playing for England and I suspected a bit of treachery afoot when both of our openers went very cheaply. I came to the crease and hit 17 runs off my first over, only to be clean bowled off the first ball of the next. It was a batter's pitch. Trouble was our team didn't have any. Australia's bowlers had obviously played before and were giving us grief, but it was the heat that really caused the problems. In the shade it was 47°C, while out in the sun it was well over 50°C. By the time our last wicket fell we had amassed a very ordinary score of 78 runs.

If batting had been hard in the heat, fielding was horrible. You could feel your skin searing. Luckily for us it only took Australia seven overs and two wickets to hit 79 runs, but the real miracle was that the game ended just as the pub re-opened!

We returned to the pub and continued where we left off, 20 of us sitting around the bar in a big crescent. The money was pooled on the bar and the barman refilled our glasses after nearly every mouthful, as is common in Western Australia. At that time they used a four-ounce glass in many public bars, known as a Pony. I don't know why, but these drinks had a shocking habit of slowly catching up on you. As we settled down, a Geordie lad took over the conversation, regaling us with hilarious stories of things he'd never done in places he'd never been.

All the men kept one ear on the conversation and one eye on the round. They were excellent company, and as the evening wore on we got slowly hammered. It reached a point where I knew I had had enough, when Geordie asked me a question. I thought I knew the answer but it came out ... 'Zbrillyzhip ... sublum ...' I hadn't spoken for about an hour and my lips were no longer responding. Those little four-ounce glasses do that.

Silence followed. 'What?' Geordie asked with a grin, aware of my state. I vainly attempted to say something else until I fell apart laughing. Then I slid off the stool as my legs had given up as well. And that was about it for Christmas Day.

The next morning, despite being a wee bit delicate, we got away early. Brad's EH managed to behave itself for most of the trip home. We only had one unscheduled stop at a creek crossing, and had a swim as his car cooled down and we made it back to Hedland just in time to be called out to fix a breakdown in the screen house. It took us all night to fix— overtime that paid for our Christmas in Marble Bar.

13

Happy New Year

On New Year's Eve Denny invited us all to his place for a party. He was the only one of us who was married, and he lived with his wife Sheryl and three young sons in the new suburb of South Hedland. Also camped at his place were his mother-in-law, two sisters-in-law and a brother-in-law, so there were nine of them altogether in a three bedroom terraced house. Nice and cosy was how Denny described it.

At the party in Den's back yard, Sheryl's sisters, 16 year-old Karen and Pat, 18, were dressed to impress, which spelt trouble. I felt tension in the air as a lot of locals were wandering around and sure enough, long before midnight, a gang of youths tried to gate crash the party. Although they were successfully repelled they threatened to return with a bigger group. This provoked Denny's brother-in-law Billy who jumped the fence and steamed into about half a dozen of them with a large plank of wood.

Believing the scrum was developing into a knife fight, a neighbour called the police who arrived just as Billy was delivering his *coup de gras*. They tossed him into the back of the caged paddy wagon alongside another couple of fellas, and we didn't like the odds.

Most of the coppers in places like Port Hedland are bullies and thugs who are based there because it's the end of the line for them. In this situation, when they started pushing their weight around, our tough screen house crew proved more than a match for them.

Hopelessly outnumbered, they failed to stop us getting Billy out of the back of the paddy wagon, but soon returned with reinforcements in riot gear and split a few heads, Karen's included. Her mother lost the plot and for the next few minutes, young and old, we gave an excellent account of ourselves.

In the end the cops managed to lock up Den, Billy, and Billy's mum in the paddy wagon, and we were ordered to disperse. Karen needed stitches, and Sheryl and Denny's three boys went with her to the hospital while most of our lads returned to the camp. I found myself alone with Pat in the kitchen, just like I'd planned. We were both pretty drunk and when midnight came around I kissed her Happy New Year and she responded quite warmly. 'Happy New Year,' I repeated to myself as she led me up the stairs. Well, someone had to keep her company.

14

Andy's invention

1973 was over and I believed that my relationship with Elaine had also died. I was still receiving what I'll call nice letters from her, but less frequently, and I wasn't replying as quickly as I struggled to find the words that used to flow so easily.

The subject of Elaine coming out and joining me never arose, and of course the night with Pat indicated that changes were happening. Despite the fact that I couldn't bring myself to tell Elaine our relationship was over, it was inevitable that the time and distance would cause our hearts to wander and for me that process had already started.

We were known to the police after that New Year's Eve fracas, so most of us kept a low profile. I worked almost every day in January 1974, one of the hottest months on record when temperatures continually approached the 40°C mark, and we almost melted in the sweltering conditions.

A tiny oasis in our existence was a trip to an air-conditioned office. This rarely happened as people hardly wanted someone like me dripping mud all over their floor, but it did happen, and on one such occasion I stood dripping mud over the desk as well as the floor of our superintendent Andy Hall's office.

Andy, a fat, bald man with beady eyes and National Health glasses, had invented a tool to align two pulleys. For fitters like me this tool had always been a piece of string, but our foreman Stan Brown told me Andy had designed something that was going to revolutionise our work.

He got up from behind his desk and opened the case he had made to house the instrument, which gleamed all chrome and stainless against the green baize lining. It looked impressive, yet I wondered how practical it was.

Andy, I was told, was responsible for maintaining the Port facility and overseeing all the financial aspects. He gave me a brief description of how his invention worked before I beat a hasty retreat. Much as I liked the air conditioning I found him rude, and he made me feel uncomfortable.

I took his invention down to the screen house floor where Den and Jimmy were waiting for me.

'So this is it?' asked Den. As I placed the case on the top step and opened it, I could see he was as impressed with the package as I had been.

'How does it work?' Jimmy wanted to know. A small crowd was now starting to gather.

'I haven't the remotest idea,' I told him. I clamped, screwed, unscrewed and adjusted and, well, after 10 minutes of struggling with the thing I asked Stan to call Andy. We rarely saw Andy on the screen floor and when Jimmy saw him waddling down through the dust he disappeared quickly upstairs with Frank and Brad leaving me to face our bad-tempered boss all on my own. He wasn't best pleased.

'I thought you knew what you were doing.' He snapped.

'I'm sorry Archie, but, it doesn't look right. It doesn't look like it can work like this.' I explained.

'Where's the other blade?' He asked tersely. He was already starting to sweat quite profusely: dark stains appeared on his khaki shirt and perspiration covered his face.

'The blade is here, but where does it fit?' I asked. There was a massive bang right above our heads and dust rained down on the small group of us standing around the screen motor.

'You've got to slide that in there as I told you,' he indicated vaguely, sweat dripping off the end of his nose and chin.

Bang! Another cloud of dust fell. Andy looked up. 'What the fuck are they doing up there?' he asked irritated.

'Liner change in the feeder,' Denny lied, 'I'll go and tell them to stop.' He couldn't get away quick enough: the dust was choking.

'Show me where this blade fits,' I persisted. Archie's glasses had slid down to the end of his nose and dust and sweat were in his eyes as his pudgy little fingers tried to undo a screw.

Bang! Another liner hit the floor above us and more dust fell. Archie removed his hard hat and tried again to loosen the screw. Just at the crucial moment when everything was loose another wear plate crashed to the floor above causing Archie to drop the rod, a clamp and two blades. They bounced off the chute wall below on to the fines conveyor and off to Japan.

Andy was incensed. 'AAAAAGGGHHHHH FUCK IT! USE A PIECE OF STRING!' he yelled, picking up his hard hat and stomping off back to his office. I headed up to the feeder floor where Jimmy and Brad were still dropping plates.

'You can stop it now, he's gone.' I told them.

Brad threw his wear plate onto the floor and looked at me.

'Wanna piece of string?'

'I think so.'

15

The strike

January turned into February, but it didn't get any cooler. On the evening of every third day I took my sodden mass of filthy rags to the laundry, but since Christmas there had been fewer and fewer working washing machines available. It got to the stage where I had to drop my self-imposed ban on going into town in order to buy some more clothes.

If any grievances at all became serious enough to be discussed casually in the mess, such as the poor quality food, the lack of washing machines and driers or broken TVs, you could bet your house that the union would pick up on it and act. The day after I bought my new wardrobe a 'stop work' meeting was called to discuss the washing machine problem.

In the six months that I had worked there, we had been out on strike twice. Once it was because Brother Steve was sacked for flattening Brother Bob with a fork lift and was lucky he wasn't put away. The other stoppage was because the quality of the food in the mess at that time was crap.

These days the quality of life in any mining camp in Australia is second to none. Everyone has his or her own room, complete with ensuite facilities, a television and Internet access, whereas in those days we shared rooms, toilets and showers and a TV room that showed the ABC. The food these days is as good as you will eat anywhere, with seafood nights once or twice a week (I once heard someone exclaim 'Lobster Thermidor again!') It was a far cry from 1974 when our camp cooks were skilled in 18 ways to cook mince.

The changes brought in over the past 30 years now mean that everyone who works in the mining industry can live a comfortable, normal life. And why shouldn't they? Although today's rosters are usually down to days away rather than weeks, most workers are still away from family and friends for extended periods. In the old days you went to those places and stayed until you'd had enough. Something had to change, and I like to think that I had something to do with it.

That February morning we stood out in the sun while our union leaders complained about the general conditions in the camp. The washing machines were mentioned, the need for more single rooms was on the agenda and a couple of other issues were raised. They gave us a bit of ammunition to take to management, but I noticed that there were a dozen or so boats on trailers in the car park—a pretty good indication we were going out for a couple of days regardless of what the issues were. Sure enough, when it came to a vote, we decided unanimously to go out the gate for 48.

The *West Australian* reported the strike the next day. They mentioned the list of conditions but it was the washing machines that they really picked up on.

'Iron Men of the North West Demand More Washing Machines' was the banner headline designed to belittle us. I wrote a letter to the editor of the *West Australian*. I asked him how long he could do my job without a washing machine when, after 10 hours in the screen house, your clothes were drenched, sodden rags and after three days there was no such thing as your cleanest dirty shirt. I wrote a long account of the working conditions in the screen house and said the newspaper's headline was an attempt to belittle us. To their credit they published my letter.

So inevitably we went out on strike. Those guys who had family in Perth or down south went home while the rest of us hung around town like a bad smell. The first couple of days were a novelty and Adam and I went to the pool and played a bit of football. But with all of us having too much time on our hands we were bound to get into trouble.

I came into the mess on the third morning and found my crew having breakfast—everyone except Jimmy. Apparently he'd received an unwelcome visitor.

'Seems like he got a knock on the door last night from an old friend,' Davie from Paisley told me.

'Out here? You don't really get people just passing do you?'

Then, right on cue Jimmy and his visitor ambled into the mess and Jackie McDonald was introduced.

Jackie, believe it or not, was Scottish. As I looked around the tables I realised that of the 10 of us sitting in there that morning I was the only non-Jock.

'Ah, another Sweaty, that's all we need,' I said by way of an ice breaker.

'What's that s'posed to mean?' Jackie asked, bristling.

'Whatever you want it to mean, Jimmy,' I laughed, taking an instant dislike to him.

'The name is Jackie.'

'I know. I was talking to Jimmy.' I got up from the table: as far as I was concerned breakfast was over.

I purposely stayed on my own for the next couple of days. We lived in each other's pockets 24/7 and I have always valued a bit of time to myself. I was lucky in having my own car and being able to take off whenever I liked, so that morning I jumped in the car and without announcing my intentions to anyone, drove off to Cossack, a ghost town about one hundred kilometres down the road. I had to ford the Sherlock River again, but since I'd lived in the North West for six months now and was used to these river crossings, the river didn't offer any challenge at all this time.

The Whim Creek Hotel appeared like a mirage. I came around a corner heading south and there was a hotel in the middle of nowhere. 'No signpost. This'll do,' I thought to myself. I pulled into the small car park to be greeted by a camel, and in fact I ended up having a drink with him. I bought a can and the barman said 'D'you wanna buy him one?' gesturing toward the camel who had stuck his head through the open window.

'Is he old enough to drink?'

'I think he's about both our ages combined.'

'What does he drink?'

'Anything except West End. No-one drinks that.'

So I bought a can of Emu, opened the window and put the can on the window sill for the camel who picked it up with his mouth, took a sip and replaced it on the sill. I'd never seen that before nor since.

I had two beers there, bought the camel a roadie, and went on my way. Of the various animals they have had drinking at the Whim Creek Hotel over the years, the funniest was a kangaroo that would get drunk and hop across the lawn. He'd start on both feet but developed a serious list and would hop a bit further on one leg before crashing into the rose garden.

I think either the RSPA or Alcoholics' Anonymous must have got involved because there are no more drunken animals at the hotel any more, well none with four legs at any rate.

It's a short drive from Whim Creek to Roebourne where you turn off for the coast. Cossack is an old mine site with the remains of the small town that used to be there—an interesting part of the world. I walked through the deserted streets, the wind whipping up the dust and sand, and I found myself sheltering in a doorway until the flurry passed. The hairs on my neck and arms stood up: I felt a sense of something. In fact the whole place had an eerie feel to it. I felt that I walked back to the car a bit too quickly.

I drove down the road a bit further and came to Point Samson, the end of the road and an excellent place to stop. I caught sight of a small pub with a restaurant on the roof that was about as busy as Cossack had been. Funny, I had come to this place to get away from people, yet as soon as I got there I wanted to share it with someone.

I thought how Elaine would have liked this beautiful location and I decided to spend the night in a room at the pub. I walked for miles along the beach without spying a single person. I hoped that someone else might have arrived by the time I got back, but was disappointed to find the roof garden still deserted. I watched the sun go down, ordered tea, drank a few more beers and had an early night. I became quite depressed. I wanted to be on my own but this wasn't what I needed.

At dawn I was back on the road to Hedland and I returned to camp to find a bit of excitement. Jimmy's mate Jackie McDonald had nicked Brad's car. It turned out he was on the run and was now being chased by our lot as well. Yesterday, when Brad, Ivan and Adam got back from drinking in town, Jackie had asked if he could borrow Brad's car. When Brad refused Jackie had given him a bit of a touch up, taken the keys and nicked the car. Brad was taken to hospital with a suspected broken cheekbone and the police and ambulance came to the camp again.

Adam and I drove up to the hospital to see how Brad was doing. We found him in a small four-bed ward with a bit of bruising and colouring but nothing serious. He was OK, just depressed. Port Hedland hospital will do that to you.

'I hope they find Jackie,' I remarked, stating the obvious. I wanted to give *him* a touch up.

'I don't.' said Brad. 'I hope he drives that car so far into the desert that they stop looking for him and then the thing breaks down. That'd be nice.' The thought caused him to smile then grimace.

A nurse came in. She was blonde and not unattractive but she wore a wedding ring.

'Are there any single nurses here?' I asked.

'A few,' she smiled.

'Where do they stay?'

'In the single nurses' quarters.'

'And that is where exactly?'

She pointed through the window. 'Over there.'

Why hadn't I thought of that before? I loved nurses. I always thought I would marry one. They were so practical and seemed to have no fear where the personal bits of the male body were concerned. Strange things always happened to them which made for remarkable conversation. Yeah, let's go and meet a couple of nurses.

We bid Brad a hasty get well and slipped over to the building across the road from the hospital. It was locked up tighter than a drum—the nurses were probably all at work or sleeping—so I wrote on a card inviting all those available to a drink tonight up at the Hedland Motel. Brilliant idea I thought.

There were three pubs in Port Hedland, the third being The Port Hedland Motel, which was new in 1974 and quite a step up in standard compared to the two in town. It sits up on a hill overlooking the ocean, on the way out of town, and I have some fond memories of relaxing on the terrace watching the sun slip into the ocean. We used to go there for the Sunday drinking session when they usually had a band in the evening. We rarely got into trouble there. It was where I took Pat on our second date.

Dating in that town was close to impossible, mainly because there were about 1,000 men to every available woman. Even when you asked a woman out you were extremely limited to the places you could take her, and if you didn't have a car you never had a date at all.

You learned never to leave your date alone, not even for a second, or a swarm of horny blokes descended. And if you thought that you might get lucky, you couldn't really bring a woman back to the camp because we all shared rooms, and if you took her home she either lived with her parents or her husband. Yes dating came with all sorts of problems, but first of all we had to meet the women.

That night four of us got dressed up and drove up to the motel to see who turned up. I'd suggested in the note that the nurses meet us at eight o'clock, and we arrived just after to find only about a dozen people in the lounge including us. (We were on strike so the whole town felt it: we couldn't spend too much as we didn't know when we were going to be paid again.) I was beginning to think that the whole exercise had been a complete waste of time, when the barmaid came across.

'Anyone here named Larry?' she asked.

'That's me.'

'Those two blokes at the bar want to talk to you.' I looked across and one of the guys raised his hand. Puzzled I made my way across to the bar.

'You blokes looking for me?'

'Yes you left a note inviting us here for a drink.'

'I didn't, I invited the nurses here for a drink.'

'We are the nurses, dear.'

16

The streaker

Eventually, after 17 days on strike, we went back to work. We got new washing machines plus a few cents an hour more, and I estimated I'd have to work there for four years before we made up the money we'd lost. So I put my head down and kept my social life to a minimum, working 10 hours a day, six days a week.

Saturday nights we'd go to the Hedland then on Sunday, our day off, we'd sleep in and enjoy a game of football. This wasn't quite as suicidal as it sounds because as the year progressed the temperatures started to drop. By April and May conditions were almost perfect for a game, even if the good done by the exercise was soon undone in the Sunday drinking session.

We were good boys for a while—until my birthday came along. I'd always taken the occasion very seriously, downing a bottle of beer for every year of my age as soon as I was old enough to drink. On May 21 1974 I became 23, one short of a carton, and a few of the lads decided to help me celebrate. Brad, Jimmy, Ivan and I drove out to Ninety Mile Beach where we started, eventually finishing up at the Hedland Motel about 12 hours later.

Streaking had become all the rage. I don't know where it started, but we'd all seen the bloke on TV streaking across the cricket pitch at Twickenham, UK, earlier in the year. No-one had done it in Port Hedland though: in this part of the world it was still a very new, very brave or very stupid thing to do.

Cheap Tuesday at the Hedland Motel brought everyone out, and by the time we got there that night there were only a few chairs left. Den and Sheryl had come along to help me celebrate and so had the rest of the lads from work. By the time we met up with them they had drunk a few and they weren't far behind us.

I talked to Adam about streaking through the pub, while Brad agreed to assist. We left the table to go to the car. The plan was I'd strip off in the top car park, come in through the back door, streak through the lounge across the dance floor and exit through the beer garden. The lads would be waiting for me in the bottom car park with my clothes in the car.

I duly stripped off and appeared at the pub door to a loud cheer, wearing only a brown paper bag on my head. The cheers became louder as I ran through the bar down the steps to the dance floor where the crowd forced me to slow my streak to a walk and I even got groped! I dived through the front door, past the startled receptionist and out into the beer garden to the car park. Unfortunately there was no car—just a busload of bewildered pensioners from Bunbury. I spotted the boys in the Charger, 100 metres away, and between me and them were the cops!

I was the first person never to be charged with streaking in Port Hedland. They were really quite good about it.

17

Beginning of the end

In June and July it's the tourist season up in the Pilbara hills. The days are usually dry and comfortably warm with clear blue skies, but as soon as the sun slips into the ocean it does get quite nippy. Brad and I were replacing a conveyor drum on one of the ship loaders when the breeze picked up and blew across the open water. For the first time in nine months I felt cold.

As we were just about finished Brad's name was called over the tannoy. He went off to answer, returning after a couple of minutes.

'The police want to speak to me.'

'What have you been up to?'

He shook his head, 'You never know with this lot—maybe guilt by association.'

'Go on, I'll finish off here.'

It was after midnight when I got back to the workshop.

'Where's Brad?' I asked Adam who had been working on another job and was washing up.

'The police have taken him. They've found Jackie

McDonald's body.'

I'd never really thought about Jackie after he disappeared. His name would come up in conversation once in a while, but as far as I was concerned he was just a nasty piece of work who seemed destined for an untimely end.

Back at the camp, we were sitting on the steps outside our donga having a beer, when Brad turned up. Something was obviously wrong.

'Jimmy and I just went to the hospital to identify Jackie McDonald. It wasn't easy.'

'Was it him?'

'Dunno. There wasn't much left of him to ID—birds and animals ate most of him. There was a wallet with his licence but ...' He faded.

'Where's Jimmy?' Adam asked.

'I don't know.' Brad shook his head, clearly in shock.

The next morning I heard Jimmy before I saw him. I was heading across to the mess for breakfast when I noticed a crowd outside and police vans and company cars parked randomly on the grass. Inside it sounded like a riot, and the voice I heard above everyone was Jimmy's.

'COME ON Y'BAS' I heard him yell.

Apparently Jimmy, Ivan and Les had been drinking all night after Jimmy had gone with Brad to identify Jackie. Jimmy blamed himself for not helping Jackie more. They'd turned up for breakfast so drunk that they were refused entry, so they decided to trash the place. Security called in the police and the riot squad turned up to subdue three men armed with jars of peanut butter. Mind you, they had done a bit of damage. Apparently those little jars can be quite lethal in the wrong hands.

That was really the beginning of the end. The three of them found themselves sacked on the spot, and were arrested for causing an affray. It was hardly a first offence for either of them: even Les, a fitter from Freo who had been with us since Easter, was known to the police. They were found guilty and ordered to pay for the damage. When they refused they were given six months in Roebourne jail. They served about half that sentence and one afternoon they were driven to Karratha airport, flown to Perth and released.

Brad, Adam, Denny and I were transferred to the ship loaders, stackers and reclaimers. On my first anniversary, I was transferred to the Cook Point single men's quarters with my own room, but it wasn't the same.

It was late October with the weather beginning to build up again and it made me wonder whether I wanted to go through another summer up here. I went into town on a warm Friday night, and in the early evening after I'd done a bit of shopping, I met up with Adam and Brad at the Esplanade. As the band was setting up, we found a table out on the edge of the beer garden close to the beach.

At the next table a group of Aboriginals—two men and two women—were doing their best to drink a jug of beer each before it got warm. I didn't pay them much attention until one of the women who was heavily pregnant got up and I was vaguely aware of a bit of commotion as the two women went down to the ocean.

Adam meanwhile was deep into a letter from his girlfriend Felicity, so deep in fact that he never noticed the crying. It seemed the woman who had been pregnant was pregnant no longer. She had just delivered her baby, returned to the table and finished her jug, as you would.

Adam looked up for a second as the baby's crying finally penetrated his world.

'Felicity's coming out.'

'She's coming here?' I asked.

'No way, I'll meet her in Melbourne.'

'When?'

'Couple of weeks.'

'You're leaving then?'

He nodded, 'I think so.'

So there it was. I went to the bar, bought a jug and

looked across at the usual scrum near the pool table. I took
the jug back to the table.

'I'll come with you. I've seen a bloke killed in this pub
and a baby born here: I think it's time to go.'

Early on the morning of the day we left, I jumped into the car
and nipped down to Nelson Point. I drove past security,
parked in the staff car park and joined the throng walking
across the dirt to the screen house. When we got to the
workshop I walked among them but knew no-one. Out of
that entire crew of 50 or so men who had been there when I
arrived, only Denny and Brad remained, and they went on to
become solid members of the Port Hedland community.

I returned to Cook Point where Adam was waiting. He
put his case and toolbox in the boot and we drove off. We
hadn't gone far when I must have strayed over the middle of
the road.

'What are you doing?' Adam complained.

'What d'you mean?'

'You're all over the road.'

'I'm just trying to see if what they say is true.'

'What's that?'

'That the best view of Port Hedland is through your
rear view mirror.'

He chuckled and moved the mirror. 'I'll look, you drive.'

18

My dad Tom

—ა&—

A few years ago I was being interviewed for a job. Part of my day was spent with someone called an industrial psychologist who went through a few preliminaries then started with his questions.

'Who were the people who influenced your formative years?'

I looked at him blankly.

'Who were your childhood heroes?'

I thought for a while before starting to roll out a familiar list:.

'Jim Morrison, John Lennon, Clint Eastwood, Harry Cripps ...' (Actually Harry Cripps was a pretty ordinary full back for Millwall whose autograph I'd once asked for somewhat awkwardly on the London tube.)

Then I really started to think about the question. Who was responsible for forming me into the person that I had become? Who influenced what I believed, what I stood for?

The answer came straight away ... my dad.

Thomas William Garner or Tom as he was known, was honest, gun barrel straight, funny, and managed to tackle everything he did with a cloak of humour.

He set his own rules. 'You never swear or use foul language in the house or in front of women. You pay your way—you always know your place in the shout. Always try to do your best. And never lie, especially to me.' These were my dad's Four Commandments.

I never heard him use a foul word in front of me, so much so I was quite concerned. Two of my old school mates went to work in the same factory as my dad and I once asked them,

'Does, my dad swear?'

'Oh yes,' said Phil, 'he's very good!' And I felt extremely pleased.

I was reminded of this some years later on one of my all too brief visits home. My cousin was playing football for Watford during the Graham Taylor/Elton John era and we were invited into the players' bar. I returned to the table after buying a round to find my dad holding court with Elton John, a couple of former England players who had recently signed for Watford, my cousin, and Graham Taylor the former England manager. My dad was about to hit the punch line when I appeared and he stalled.

'What's wrong?' asked Elton.

'I can't continue,' he said, 'me son's here.' And he refused to finish the joke.

'Come on Dad, I'm 27. I've probably heard it before.'

'Not from me you haven't.'

—ഇൽ—

19

Back on the road

Road trips, in my experience, are always eventful, and the long journey from Port Hedland to Melbourne was no exception. Adam and I left Hedland at about ten o'clock, then stopped for lunchtime refreshment at the Whim Creek Hotel where we'd become almost regulars. We had a farewell drink with the landlord, bought the camel a beer, and continued on our way.

We negotiated the Sherlock River for the last time. In the last 12 months I had done quite a bit of driving in the outback, crossing that river on more than a dozen occasions without it ever offering a real challenge. Still, I had the upmost respect for the Sherlock and I was going to miss it.

We stopped for fuel and fresh ice for the esky in Roebourne, the first town on our route. That was where the bitumen started, and we wouldn't encounter dirt again until we reached Eucla, a long way off. We got back on the road, toying with idea of nipping into Karratha for a bit of shopping, but decided that we wanted to put a good few miles behind us.

Australia is such a big country that even averaging 120 kilometres an hour we were only nibbling at the miles. Every couple of hours we stopped to stretch our legs and took turns at the wheel so the drive never became a chore. Our aim was to make it to Carnarvon by the end of the first day, but by the time we reached Lyndon River it was going dark and we'd already had a few near misses with the local wild life. Having covered 700 kilometres in seven hours, we would be in Perth by the following night, so we settled in a motel and a pub ready to enjoy the dubious delights of Lyndon River.

We were on the road by first light, arrived in Carnarvon for breakfast, Northampton for lunch and finally rolled into Perth at about half past seven. It was difficult getting used to the traffic again after driving at high speed along open roads for the past couple of days. The last hour was spent travelling at just 30 kilometres an hour through the Perth suburbs.

After we found a motel in South Perth, I tried unsuccessfully to track down Lindsay and Fred. We were staying at a nice spot on the Swan river, but with a long way still to go we didn't plan on staying any longer than a night.

Sometimes you make weak promises to yourself to revisit a certain place and sometimes you do yet there always seems to be a more attractive destination. It was probably on this trip that I decided to enjoy the journey itself.

The next day we continued our journey to Melbourne, intending to look up a mate that we'd met in Hedland on the way. Jugz Goltz lived 200 kilometres down the road in Collie, but due to a number of false starts and a puncture we didn't arrive in Collie until mid-afternoon. That meant another famous night on the ponies, those lethal five ounce glasses that creep up on you and wreak havoc.

We said goodbye to Jugz and his brothers the next morning, reached Albany in time for lunch and ended up spending that night in Esperance. It looked like our plan to be in Melbourne for the weekend wasn't going to happen. The car was playing up a bit so I worked on it in the rain most of the morning. We eventually got away at about eleven o'clock with the rain still lashing down, and reduced visibility limiting us to an average of 50 kilometres an hour. We made it to Eucla that day as I'd hoped, though not until a little after midnight.

The road from Eucla to Ceduna was the last stretch of road in Australia to be sealed with bitumen, and at the time of our journey the infamous Nullarbor Plain before us was still a strip of dirt. Instead of the usual dirt, dust and flies, however, on the day we drove across the Nullarbor there was water as far as the eye could see. The Nullarbor Sea.

We drove slowly, causing a small bow wave and taking care to avoid all sorts of little pot holes and hazards just waiting under the water to catch out an impatient driver. If we took our time through this stretch we'd get to Melbourne eventually. The trouble was, at the speed we were travelling, I didn't think we'd make Ceduna before dark.

We tootled along, entertained by a good supply of tapes and beer, occasionally passing a couple of cars going in the opposite direction. Sometimes we'd stop to compare notes with other drivers and check we were doing the right thing. Then some madman would plough through at top speed causing a massive bow wave. I wished that just one of these cretins would come unstuck, little thinking my wish would be granted.

Around mid-afternoon as I was driving through continuing heavy rain with visibility deteriorating even further, an XW suddenly flew past, scaring the life out of me and just about swamping us. The driver was gone as quickly as he arrived, disappearing into the rain.

'What a complete idiot,' cursed Adam.

The rain continued to fall and by about five o'clock, as it was starting to get quite gloomy, I saw some tail lights of a car ahead of us. It was the red XW whose driver was waving us down.

'Am I glad to see you.' he said cheerfully.

'Well, well, it's Fangio. What have you done?' Adam

asked from the passenger seat, the driver looked in, first at me than at Adam.

'I think I did a bit of damage back at the cattle grid back there.'

'You're a fool,' Adam declared, with no effort to hide his contempt.

'I'm in a hurry.'

'Not any more you're not.' I told him.

'I've got to be in Adelaide tomorrow.'

Adam and I got out of the car and had a good look at the Falcon. He had almost managed to rip the front axle right off, the front wheels had been forced back against the back of the wheel arch, and both tyres were shredded. He wasn't going anywhere, not in that car anyway.

'You might be in Adelaide tomorrow, but this thing won't,' I told him.

'Can you give me a tow?'

'You need a tow truck.'

'But I can't leave it here; it will be stripped by the time I get back with a tow truck.'

'And all of a sudden this is our problem?' I asked.

'Well you can't leave me here.'

'I won't leave you here but I'm not towing your car.'

'I'd leave you here.' Adam put in.

'The way I see it you have two choices; you can stay here and we'll tell the nearest tow truck where you are, or you can come with us and take your chances. Make up your mind because we have places we have to be too.'

He dithered for few seconds before deciding, much to Adam's annoyance, to join us. A bit further down the road we came across another casualty who had been heading west but accepted our offer of a lift back to Ceduna. So here we were with two fools who'd been driving with no consideration whatsoever for the road conditions, both of them commenting on how slow we were driving.

'Faster than walking,' Adam said.

We eventually arrived in Ceduna at six o'clock the next morning exactly 24 hours after we left Eucla. The sea of water seemed to disappear almost as soon as we hit the bitumen. We left Fangio and his mate in search of a tow truck and had breakfast at a roadhouse before washing down the car and continuing on our way.

The rain eased and as we headed east the road slowly started to get busier. We were tired and called stumps at lunch time in Port Augusta where we spent all of the next day pulling everything out of the car and washing away all traces of the Nullarbor dirt. We found a pub close by that sold West End, without doubt the second worst beer in the world, (the worst being that other South Australian drop Southwarks). The beer is possibly one of the reasons why I have never worked in South Australia and still have no desire to go there.

From Port Augusta we headed for Melbourne via the Great Ocean Road. A more direct route through Horsham was possible but we both liked the idea of the scenic drive more. It was a pleasant drive but soon we were growing a bit sick of driving and wanted to get to Melbourne. If we made one last stop in Princetown that night we thought we'd be there the following day.

The bright clear weather in the morning brought with it an optimism that I had been looking for since leaving Perth nine days ago. We flew past the Twelve Apostles and Lorne, aware we were not far from our final destination. Adam was driving as we passed through the western suburbs of Melbourne with the windows down and the music up. We'd reached the end of the road.

20

Joining the hippies

We found the house on Newry Street quite easily, led by the noise. Although it wasn't exactly a warm day the door and all the front windows were open. Shirtless, and quite worse for wear from too many beers, Ivan and Les from Freo greeted Adam and I like long lost brothers and we were soon joined by Jimmy and a dozen other people who swarmed out on our arrival. It wasn't lunchtime yet but everyone was blotto.

Right across the road was the Lord Nelson, a very handy watering hole that also sold take-away food. I went across the road and asked the barman for a cold carton.

He shook his head. 'Nothing cold left—the hippies over the road have cleaned us out.'

Apparently I was going to become one of the 'hippies over the road' whether I liked it or not. I bought a couple of bottles of wine and returned to find that the bathtub was already full of booze. So was the fridge and so was an esky in the back yard.

'When that runs out there's this lot too,' Ivan proudly

declared, showing me another half a dozen cartons in a cupboard under the stairs.

'What's the occasion?'

'Er ... no reason, just an excellent opportunity to get legless.'

Newry Street, North Fitzroy, Melbourne, Victoria, had been our final destination when we set off from Port Hedland 10 days ago, but now I was here it stung of anticlimax. Once again I thought the journey had been so much more rewarding than the arrival, and I got the impression Adam was feeling the same as I caught a glimpse of him trying to reason with some nonsense Ivan was spouting.

I sat in the concrete backyard of the old Victorian house. It was going to be worth a small fortune in a few years with yuppies looking for low maintenance places close to the city, but it didn't do anything for me. I drank straight from the bottle, listening to Jerry who hated everybody and saw no value in anything.

These ramblings were going on all over the place, very animated as drunken conversations tend to be. I was desperately trying to catch the eye of a tiny woman who seemed to be hovering on the edge of about three conversations.

'That's Carol,' Jerry told me when he realised I was more interested in her than in what he had to say. He called her over.

'Carol this is Larry.'

'I know,' she said, 'I saw you arrive.'

She was barely five feet tall with long chestnut hair and an impish face that I found extremely attractive, and I could see her pert little breasts through the white cheesecloth blouse that she nearly wore. With her long, aqua blue sarong and no shoes she could easily be described as the hippie over the road. Jerry wandered off leaving me to find my own way with her. I asked her if she wanted a drink.

'I don't drink alcohol.'

'Would you like a soft drink, fruit juice?'

'No, I'm fine.' She seemed out of place.

'So when you're not being a hippy what do you do?' I asked.

'I'm a nurse at the Mercy Hospital.' She must be older than she looked.

I noticed there were at least a dozen blokes and three women—the same old disproportionate number as there'd been in Port Hedland.

'D'you fancy showing me around Melbourne?' I asked.

'When?'

'How about right now?'

She took about a second to decide and a minute later we were driving down Nicholson Street in my car, its carpets still covered in red dust from Western Australia. As we passed the Exhibition Buildings, there were dozens of cars parked outside. The motor show was on and at another time I would have stopped. I'll go next year I thought absently.

In the city I negotiated my first right hand turn. Melbourne is the only city in the entire universe where you go to the left to turn right, and turning left isn't much easier. It was a very nervous first hour, but by the time we drove past the Melbourne Cricket Ground I had the car and the unique road rules under control-ish.

She took me out to St Kilda where we parked the car and went for a walk along the beach and out along the Pier. On this beautiful spring afternoon Carol was the ideal host. We had a drink at the Beaconsfield Hotel on the Esplanade and I fell in love with the place. I hadn't been here a day, but I was already making plans to live in this part of town.

We walked back to the car, returning to the city via Port Melbourne and South Melbourne. Over Princes Bridge I spotted Young & Jackson's or Chloe's.

'We have to have a drink in here.'

'Why's that?' Carol asked innocently.

'It's the most famous pub in Melbourne.'

Though she'd lived in Melbourne all of her life she had

never heard of it.

Carol was a really attractive young woman who would have turned heads in most pubs but everyone in this one seemed to be gawking at her in a non-too-welcoming way. We quickly realised she was the only woman in the bar so we drank up and made a quick exit.

21

A bit of bovver

Carol led me across the busy road from Flinders Street Station down Swanston Street. We found a little wine bar, sat at a table across from each other and swapped stories. She was 22, and having recently finished her nurses' training, now worked at the Mercy Hospital in East Melbourne. She lived in the nurses' quarters there during the week, returning home to Bentleigh at the weekend.

She was easy to talk to, laughed readily, and I found myself attracted to her. Apart from a couple of disastrous dates in Port Hedland, this was the first time in a while that I had actually sat down with a woman and I just enjoyed Carol's company.

We talked for ages and it was dark when we finally left the bar.

'So where to next?' I asked her.

'Can you take me back to my digs? I have an early shift tomorrow.'

Reluctantly I agreed to take her home, but as we got to the car the ground seemed to come up to meet me. I realised I hadn't eaten since breakfast and we had just downed a couple of bottles of wine not to mention the few beers I'd consumed during the course of the day. Now the alcohol was having a profound effect on me.

With the rush hour over, the streets were easy to navigate but the further we went the worse I got and as we drove down Wellington Parade I had one eye closed.

In the 60s and early 70s when it wasn't against the law to drive under the influence, I used to find that closing one eye was a massive aid and usually a pretty good indication that you should either stop soon or drive faster to get to your destination quicker.

'Are you ok to drive back to Fitzroy?' Carol asked when we pulled up outside her digs.

'Asabutely.' I told her 'Where is it?'

I forgot her directions the second I drove away from the kerb and for the next hour or so I drove around Melbourne totally lost and totally drunk.

At about ten o'clock I was eventually pulled over by a police car. I don't really know what happened next except that apparently I gave them a mouthful of abuse and was nabbed for being drunk and disorderly. I was taken to Russell Street police station where I was pushed into a steel cabinet, shut in, and then rolled all over the place.

It was scary. I was turned upside down, smashed onto my face, then thrown feet first into the concrete. The back of my head slammed against the inside wall of the cabinet, I threw up, my nose was bleeding and a cut opened up over my eye. Bang, bang, bang, crash, roll, smash .... It went on for a long time until eventually they got tired, opened the locker door and I fell out in heap on the floor covered in my own blood and vomit. Finally they took me out the back, put the hose on me and threw me in the tank for the night. Quite a sobering experience!

I was woken up the next morning by the duty sergeant who took me to a room where I was given my watch and wallet back. I felt I'd gone ten rounds with Rocky.

'Now,' said the sergeant, 'I'd like to know if anyone laid a finger on you last night?'

I shook my head. 'No, not a soul.'

'Do you want to make a complaint about how you were treated last night?'

'No.' I just wanted to get out of the police station as quickly as possible.

'Then sign here please sir and I trust we won't be seeing you again.'

'You've got my word on that.'

He told me my car was on Victoria Street and showed me the door. I didn't have a clue where Victoria Street was, but didn't stop to enquire. I asked directions of two people outside who gave me very short shrift. Catching sight of my reflection in a shop window I could hardly blame them.

My car, when I eventually found it, was a sight for sore eyes—and sore legs. I was about to get in when a guy came out of a newsagents' shop.

'Can you tell me where Newry Street is mate?'

'You look like shit,' he replied. And he was gone.

I went into the newsagents and obtained directions from the shop assistant, but only after she told me I looked like shit and should be ashamed of myself.

'I *am* ashamed of myself. I've just been released from jail and I'm not in a very good mood but I promise if you direct me I'LL GET OUT OF YOUR LIFE FORFUCKINEVER.' A few minutes later I was driving past the now-familiar Exhibition Buildings on my way back to my new home.

The front door was open, there were bodies everywhere and out the back I found the remnants of the party. Ivan, Jimmy and Les from Freo were sitting talking Scottish gibberish until they saw me.

'Larry, you look like shit man,' Ivan told me.

'It's a common observation.'

22

Steve

The *Saturday Age* is a wonderful newspaper if you are looking for a job as we were, well, as I was. Ivan and Adam had already decided they were heading back to Scotland. Jimmy was undecided as was Les and there was a general disinterest in the idea of working anyway.

I must admit we did look like hippies. Ivan with his hair to his shoulders rarely wore a shirt or shoes and I never saw him wash, but then again I like to think he didn't spend much time watching me wash either. We all wore beards and there was a general air of unkemptness about us.

At any one time at least 10 people stayed at the house. The front door was rarely closed and there was a continual dope-infused party atmosphere. So when I brought the *Age* home one morning there was no interest in the job columns and the paper was used to fire up the barbecue.

I couldn't continue living there—it was hard work. I never slept in the same bed two nights in a row. Those of us with money were supposed to support those with none, but when those with none got their dole they disappeared.

I wanted a job and a place of my own.

I had been staying at the house for a week when the chaotic conditions finally got to me. That's it, I thought, I'm out of here. As I was getting my things together Steve came in. Unlike most of the others Steve had a real job, but it wasn't until that evening that I found out what a cracking little number he had.

'Can you give me a ride to work?' he asked. 'I put my car in for a service and it won't be ready until tomorrow.'

Then he saw me packing. 'What are you doing?'

'I'm leaving. If I stay here any longer I'll either catch something or hit someone.' I went looking for Adam to say goodbye but he seemed to have transferred to his brother's place in Notting Hill so I moved out without telling anyone.

Steve worked for the ABC. He was a news editor, and by all accounts quite a good one. We drove across town to Elsternwick, arriving at the ABC Ripon Lea Studios at six thirty. Steve's job was to get the news stories ready for the Seven O'clock News.

'You are on the air at seven and you start now?' I asked in amazement.

'No, I won't start until about ten to seven when they decide which story will lead. Then, while the news is on, I cut and edit it a few minutes before it appears on the telly.'

'Incredible.'

He had a lot of fun with it too. On the night I was there he cut and taped the footage together for a story about the local sheepdog trials. At the end, instead of showing the winner, the clip featured a hapless owner whose dog had lost the plot screaming 'you bastard' at the heavens. I'm sure it brought a smile to the face of everyone who saw it.

Half an hour later we were over the road enjoying a drink at the Elsternwick Hotel.

'And that's your job?'

'Pretty much.'

'Half an hour a day?'

'Twenty five minutes actually!'

There was just one more party to attend before I could put a bit of distance between me and the hippies over the road. Ivan and Adam were flying back to Scotland and it just wouldn't do to drop them off at Tullamarine airport on the way to work in the morning. Oh no, we had to have a cast of thousands.

Adam and I came to Melbourne because I thought he was going to meet up with his girlfriend and live here, but something had happened and all bets were off. His farewell party was not unlike many celebrations in Newry Street with plenty of booze, (we cleaned out Lord Nelson again), plenty of women, (we phoned every nurses' hostel in town) and plenty of illegal drugs.

It was only a question of time before the place got busted and I didn't want to be around when it did. The party went on from just after mid-day until about nine o'clock in the evening when we poured ourselves into the cars and took Adam and Ivan to the airport.

It was organised chaos. We lost Ivan; Adam went with his brother; I took half a dozen, Steve transported another crowd in his BMW—hippies in a Beamer! In the midst of the havoc we caused at the airport I did manage a few final words with Adam. Although we had been good mates in Port Hedland, we hardly saw each other once we got to Melbourne as he was more reluctant than I to make Newry Street home. We said a stiff goodbye before I slipped out the back door.

From what I could make out from Steve, a couple of days later, Ivan missed the plane and he and Jimmy flew out the next day. Les got locked up for being drunk and disorderly and they found some gear on him that inevitably led to a raid on the house the next day. He and Jeanie got busted and were sent down for a year.

A couple of weeks later, when I found myself in Fitzroy, I nipped into the Lord Nelson for a swift one and asked for half a dozen to go. Noticing the glass door fridge was full I chuckled to myself. We might have been the hippies over the road but I think they missed us.

Steve was a member of the ABC's VFL football team which played in a charity league with Channel o, Channel 7, Channel Nine, The Age, and, for some reason, the Australian airline Qantas.

Every Sunday towards the end of the year we played a game of Aussie Rules football. It was very well advertised and TV personalities from the various Channels would turn out to play and get their photo taken with Joe or Joan public to raise money for a good cause.

Bellbird was the pick of the ABC soaps at the time while The Box and 96 were also at the height of their popularity so there was a lot of public interest in the stars of these shows playing football.

Despite the big crowds of spectators, the team's manager Dave always complained that he could never get enough players. When he asked me if I would be interested I jumped at the chance of becoming a regular for them. I needed a crash course in Aussie Rules so Steve and I went over to the park with a couple of friends to practice.

A few days later on a pleasant Sunday afternoon, Steve picked me up to take me out to Croydon Football Club where the team from ABC were to play a match with Channel 9. The opposing team included TV personalities Ernie Sigley, Denise Drysdale and Bert Newton.

It was a diverting way to spend a couple of hours, during which I suffered the thoroughly enjoyable experience of having Denise fall on top of me! I consumed four beers in the first quarter of the match, three in the second, and two at half time, followed by three in the third quarter and three in the fourth.

At the end of the game I was approached by an official of Croydon Football Club.

'You are incredible.'

'Thanks very much,' I agreed.

'D'you want to come here?'

'Play here?' I asked.

'Play? No. If you could just appear in our bar every night our takings would go through the roof. And if you could bring him along,' he said pointing to Steve who was being violently ill behind the club house, 'we'd really appreciate it.'

Considering Steve and I lived in a part of Oz where Sunday drinking was banned, I thought we'd done quite well.

23

My dad from Rovrive

—ഓരു—

Thomas William Garner was born on June 29 1922 under the sign of Cancer, and when he died two weeks shy of his 79th birthday, cancer was probably the only thing not listed as his possible killer. No-one should have experienced what my dad endured during his last few years.

Tom was a Cockney from Rotherhithe, the dockland slum he would describe as a quaint little village on the south bank of London's River Thames. He had a bit of trouble pronouncing the 'th' so Rotherhithe was always *Rovrive*. Occasionally, when he found himself in company, it was amusing to watch him try to get his false teeth around Rotherhithe. Wapping, down the road, was so much easier.

I disliked our former prime minister, Margaret Thatcher, more than any other UK politician, but the one good thing she did was to free people from the shackles of renting and allow them to buy their own council houses.

On our North London council estate my dad had paid

rent for the best part of 30 years until one day the Thatcher government decided it didn't want to pay for the upkeep of these houses any more. We were told, 'If you want to, you can buy them, and you can look after them.'

A value was put on the property and if the rent you had paid over the years met the value, you got your house for nothing. Our house, 26 Stretton Way, was worth £7200 in 1980 and by the time he became its owner my dad had already paid for it twice over in rent. His pride shone through in the letter he sent me saying he was finally living in a home that was his. I was so pleased for him.

One of the many things I regret never having bought him was a house nameplate with *Rovrive* on it. What better name could there have been for his home?

—⌘—

24

Dry Sundays

My fortunes were picking up. I had moved into a nice little single bedroom flat in St Kilda, far from the maddening crowd in Newry Street. I had also landed a job as a welder on the Loop, the underground link being built under the city of Melbourne. I worked for a contracting company, installing the signals through the 16 kilometres of tunnel—a good little number close to the centre of a very vibrant city.

My work mates were pretty good value too. I was working with Ross and Kevin Costner, two brothers who knew Melbourne like the back of their hand. I spent quite a few weekends with them in the Mount Erica Hotel, their favourite watering hole in Prahran where they lived.

After finishing work on a Saturday afternoon we would head for either Princess Park to watch Carlton, the Costner boys' team, or for Moorabbin to watch St Kilda, the team that I adopted before changing my allegiances to the Saints. You have to support a team in Melbourne, otherwise you are treated as something of a leper.

After the game we would make our way back to Prahran and the Erica.

One evening, Kevin asked me out of the blue what I was doing the following morning. 'Hopefully I won't be awake for most of it. Why?'

'Fancy a beer?'

'On a Sunday? Chance would be a fine thing.' In Victoria, until the late 1980s, there was nowhere to get a drink legally on a Sunday without buying a meal.

'There's a good chance,' said Kevin, and he went on to tell me about the Sunday Suckers.

Apparently every Sunday since 1945, these blokes had been driving over to the brewery in Carlton to pick up an 18 gallon keg, together with hoses and all the fittings. They had taken these to carefully selected places for secret drinking sessions. These meetings used to be restricted to just the original members but apparently the older ones were dropping off, and new blood was needed.

As a Pom I took it as quite an honour to be asked to join this exclusive club.

'Yeah I'd love to. Where, how, when?'

'Pick me up tomorrow at about nine thirty and I'll tell you.'

The following day I picked up Kevin and Ross and we drove to an address near Armadale station used by the Sunday Suckers. We arrived early to help them set up.

It was all very Mason-ish with the old fellas of the higher order sitting around the back yard being waited on by the youngsters. Kevin, at almost 40, was definitely considered a youngster. The notable absence of women was hardly surprising since no women were allowed to be members nor ever invited as guests.

Kev explained that the drinking bouts were held at different locations that fitted the Sunday Suckers' requirements. A back yard was needed big enough to cater for as many as 50 people at a time. (I thought 18 gallons wouldn't go far among 50 but I kept my opinion to myself.) There had to be an outside urinal plus some kind of shelter in case of bad weather.

Over the years, about eight places had been selected that met these vital criteria. Each of the senior members sat in his regular spot and woe betide anyone who took the wrong chair.

I felt awkward, like a person who had joined a club without knowing the rules. On more than one occasion I was told that I was one of a very small group of Poms who had been given the privilege of an invitation and I thanked them for the opportunity. It all seemed rather odd though.

On this occasion a guest speaker addressed us—a member who seemed to travel a lot. He spoke well, and without doubt was worth the time, but all too quickly he finished his little narrative. We refilled our glasses, toasted the Queen and that was about it. By mid-day the keg was empty.

I was invited back one Sunday morning about three weeks later. I went along with Ross again, on this occasion to a location on Williams Street where all the houses appeared to have been built just after the Second World War. They were all similar and were ageing, like their owners.

I felt as awkward as I had on my previous visit. There was another guest speaker, but this one didn't hold my attention like the speaker last time had done. Just after mid-day the Queen was duly toasted, the keg drained and again I found myself walking back to the car wondering what this was all about.

The following week I received a phone call from Ross and was ready to say no thanks to any suggestion of another Sunday Suckers' session, when he asked me to pick up the keg from the brewery. This was an honour never before bestowed on a Pom, so I humbly accepted.

Everything would have been hunky dory except the day before that Sunday Suckers' meeting I had a late night and missed some important public information. Steve and I went over to a restaurant on Lygon Street for a meal with Gerry and Joan, friends we had met when I first came to Melbourne. Because Joan and Gerry had an almighty bust up in the restaurant, I ended up seeing Joan home and it was late when I arrived back to my flat in St Kilda.

I woke up the next morning just after nine and phoned Ross but there was no answer. After dressing, eating a bit of breakfast and phoning again without success I decided to go on my own to pick up the keg. I drove over to the brewery, only to find the place closed. This was terrible, I thought, but I couldn't help chuckling. Kevin had told me the Sunday Suckers never missed a session.

I was in the car listening to the radio and wondering what to do next when the twelve o'clock news came on. 'Twelve o'clock!' I said to myself. Then it dawned on me that the clocks had gone forward during the night: daylight saving had started.

I did a quick circuit around the brewery one more time but I knew that it was no use. I'd missed it. Sorry lads.

Fortunately Steve and I had a game against Channel Nine arranged for two o'clock in Thomastown. I would still get a drink this Sunday but I knew a few who wouldn't.

25

Next stop Sydney

It was late spring, a little before seven in the morning as I edged through the traffic towards Jollimont Railway Yard. The hourly rate I was paid working on the Loop underground system was quite impressive because it included the same underground allowance as miners received. Fortunately I wasn't in some isolated mine site but in Melbourne and I could come up in the middle of the city any time I liked for lunch, smoko or anything.

It was what I called a hobby job, something to do until more lucrative work came along. It was ideal and with a nice place to live and a quality car and I felt there was only one little piece of the puzzle missing. It could only be a question of time before someone came along to make my life brighter than it already was. I was in a good mood on this beautiful morning watching the girls making their way to work. I raced down Wellington Parade, pulled into the yard car park and clocked in.

We walked through a maze of tunnels and paths to Flinders Street station where I started work installing the signals. It soon became obvious that I needed a lot of gear to keep me going for the day, so I asked our easy-going foreman George Downs.

'It's all available over at the Jollimont warehouse, Lazza. They have a delivery coming this afternoon but if you're out of stuff now you can go over there and pick up what you need.'

'I won't be able to carry too much back with me,' I told him, stating the obvious.

'No, no,' George laughed. 'Come with me Lazza.'
I followed him along the tunnel to a little recess with a 'Casey Jones' handcart. I'd only ever seen them in the movies and I've never operated one.

'Give me a hand Laz,' said George.

Together we assembled the parts of the cart and in about 10 minutes it was ready for use.

'Ok, go to the top of the tunnel where you'll meet a bloke with a radio. If you tell him you want to go to Jollimont Yard he'll radio the signal box and they'll set the points for you to get across. When you get to the yard ask for Gary Lee, the fat bastard with a white beard and probably a cup of coffee in his hand. Tell him George sent you for the order. Got it?

'Gary Lee, fat bastard, beard, coffee cup.'

'That's it.'

I gave the cart a couple of pumps to find it moved fairly easily and after I gathered a bit of momentum I gave it a few more on the flat before starting the long climb up the incline to the entrance of the tunnel.

It was quite a stiff push to get to the top, and I was pleased to let the cart free wheel a bit as I rolled out into the morning air.

'Where to?' a voice enquired.' It was Eric with the radio.
'Jollimont Yard.'

'Jollimont Yard, please mate,' Eric repeated as he radioed Dave in the signal box. There was a scrambled reply and I waited for a few seconds before getting the nod.

I pushed the cart and was soon moving quite quickly as

the track levelled out. But it became obvious even to my untrained eye that I wasn't heading towards Jollimont Yard. The yard was way off to my left and there were no points to direct me to it. In fact I was heading for Richmond Station. It was just after eight on a bright Monday morning and the station was busy with school kids, business men and women who were all quite amused to see me approaching. As I pumped through the station I smiled at a couple of attractive young women.

'How're you doing?' I asked.

'Not bad,' came the giggling reply.

'Oi! Where the hell d'you think you're going?' A station worker politely asked me.

'Jollimont Yard?'

'No you're not. You're on your way to Sydney, and if you don't get your arse out of there sharpish you're gonna hit the 8:10 to Flinders Street!'

I was trying to slow the cart down but the weight of resistance was greater than mine so it only eased up a little. I eventually stopped at the far end of the platform, much to the amusement of a small crowd that had gathered.

'Can I have a ride mister?' a kid asked as I moved around to the other side of the cart and started to pump back where I'd come from. I went past the attractive young women again.

'Bet you didn't think you'd see me again so soon did you?'

They smiled.

'Wanna lift?' I asked.

'Where are you going?'

'Dunno. It depends on Dave in the signal box.'

'Maybe tomorrow,' one of them said.

'Promise?'

I was out of range, but I'm sure she said 'You gotta be joking?'

I got back and met Eric with the radio.

'I was off to Sydney.' I told him.

'I saw that. I think you'll be right now.'

This time Dave in the signal box got it right and I arrived at the warehouse at Jollimont just in time for smoko.

Gary wasn't hard to find, wedged behind his desk, cup in one hand, doughnut in the other. We had smoko and then another cup of coffee, and it was after ten when I finally got loaded ready to set off back.

Eric, who I was now on first name terms with, saw me coming and I soon negotiated the points, slipped past him into the tunnel and started to roll down the incline.

It took me only a couple of seconds to realise I might be in a little bit of bother. The cart gathered speed and I couldn't slow it down.

'Oh no!'

I looked down the long gradient and saw I was on a rollercoaster with no brakes. The cart, with the added weight of the fittings it was carrying, continued to gather speed as I peered down the track into the darkness.

'WWWAAAAA.' I said, struggling to control the thing by leaning into the pumping lever. I was thrown up like a rag doll as the cart picked up even more speed. All I could do was hang on. I bobbed up and down like a thrashing machine while the vibrations sent the brackets and boxes of nuts and bolts cascading all over the place, just a couple at first, then an avalanche.

Thump, thump, thump ... More shockwaves shot through the vehicle until the brackets bounced off the tunnel wall throwing sparks and narrowly missing me. Boxes of nuts exploded like steel confetti, spattering all over the place and still the cart went faster and faster. Now, having lost my footing completely, I resembled a flag streaming out the back of the kamikaze cart ... up and down, up and down, bang, bang, bang ... I think they heard me long before I arrived.

'WWWAAAAAAA.' I shot through Flinders Street station at about 100 miles an hour. The last of the brackets nearly decapitated George as it bounced off about three walls and ricocheted off the platform. It smashed through the waiting room window followed by a cascade of spring washers that covered the platform like shrapnel and sent people diving for cover. The platform was a blur as I vanished into the tunnel once more, this time on my way to Museum station.

'WWWAAAAAAAAAA,' I think I said.

Something broke, the lever stopped pumping and I cruised through Museum at a modest 65. Slowly, as the grade started to rise, I managed to pull myself back onto the cart and lay there until it rolled to a stop just short of Flagstaff. I sat there for a few minutes waiting to get my breath back.

'Well that was interesting.' I said to myself, realising as I hobbled back to Flinders Street that I'd hurt my knee. George and the recovery party arrived just as I was limping into Museum station.

'You alright?' George wanted to know.

'Oh yeah, mint condition.'

He laughed, relieved that my injuries weren't more serious, and tossed a triangular block of wood to me.

'What's this?' I asked inspecting the block.

'The brake,' he said.

I was taken to St Vincent's hospital for a check-up and observation and as a nurse was taking my pulse she looked at me and remarked, 'I bet you didn't expect to see me again so soon did you?' It was the attractive woman from Richmond Station ... honest.

26

Down on the farm

The nurse's name was Kathy O'Donnell. She lived in East Melbourne and we had our first date on the Friday after my incident with the 'Casey Jones' cart.

Nurses are the greatest people. In London years before, whenever we were having a party and needed a few more women, we would call the nurses' accommodation at the local hospital and always ended up with half a dozen women who were good fun and game for almost anything. I hadn't tried it in Australia except for the one occasion in Port Hedland, which wasn't exactly my finest hour. But now I had my first Australian girlfriend and I don't think it was a coincidence that she turned out to be a nurse.

Our first date was quickly followed by a second until before I knew it we were seeing each other a couple of times a week. She was from a big family in a farming community in Gippsland, a couple of hours to the south east of Melbourne. Since their father Jack had died a few years before, Kathy's brother Terry had managed the place with their sisters Pat and Fiona, while their mother Meg ran the home. Another sister, Clare, lived in Melbourne and came back at certain times of the year to help with the business.

When you went to the O'Donnells' you had to be prepared to work. There was wood to cut, dishes to wash, chickens to feed and eggs to gather. On my first visit I learned to ride the inappropriately named Storm, a lovely tempered six year-old gelding that really enjoyed being taken out.

During the muster, we had to separate the calves from the herd and then separate the male calves from the female. It was early summer and hot thirsty work but relief was at hand when Meg came out a couple of times a day with big jugs of cider and huge sandwiches. On all farms there is always a mountain of repair work to be done so when we weren't out in the paddock I'd help Terry in the garage. Being at home in a workshop I found myself in my element.

I used to go down there almost every weekend and these genuine, solid people were good to be with. We'd spend most of the day in the saddle and the evenings in the local hotel where a dance was held—good old fashioned fun. Sundays meant a little less work and more time spent with the family. I found myself getting very close to Kathy and I could have stayed there forever, except I had another agenda.

During my first year in Australia I had managed to get some work experience and a few savings behind me but I wanted to start earning real money. A job on the horizon in Bougainville, New Guinea, was offering good wages and unlimited overtime. It seemed to be exactly the opportunity I was looking for.

I applied for the position and received a letter in due course asking me to attend an interview. All this happened a few weeks before Christmas and I told them that I would be available in the New Year. I said nothing to Kathy, but with Christmas approaching I was going to be spending more time with her and I thought it would be unfair of me to have such plans going on behind her back. I decided to tell her, but she found out before I could.

Kathy had started to come over and spend the night with me in St Kilda. I gave her a key and she was almost living with me, a set up I liked. Then, the day before we were supposed to be going down to Gippsland for Christmas, she got home before me and found a big envelope in my mail box.

'What's this?' she asked.

'I don't know, I haven't opened it.' I was honest there although I did have a very good idea what it was.

Kathy was very annoyed when she learned the contents of the envelope.

'When were you going to tell me that you were going to New Guinea?'

'I've only just received confirmation that I'm going.'

'So you are going?'

'Yes.'

'And what about us?'

There it was, the 64 million dollar question. Kathy was genuinely hurt: I hadn't planned it very well and I didn't know what to say. She locked herself in my bedroom, inconsolable, and I felt like shit. I tried to explain to her that all my life I'd had nothing, that I wanted to make a new start and that this job was my chance.

When she eventually came out we sort of made up. I tried to sweeten the pill by telling her that in the long term it could be good for both of us but we knew this was the beginning of the end.

We went down to Gippsland and spent a wonderful Christmas at the O'Donnells' home with all of Kathy's extended family—mother, brother, sisters, cousins and their boyfriends, aunts and uncles. Somehow we all managed to squeeze around a large table to eat an excellent meal prepared by Meg. Bougainville was forgotten.

Our day continued with a game of backyard cricket until night fell, followed by dancing until Boxing Day. We slept where we could, waking the next morning to find Meg had cooked us a full breakfast. I would have got fat if I'd stayed there.

The temptation to stay was very great indeed: what a life I could have had. Terry had made noises about wanting someone full time in the garage. Their operation was only going to get bigger. Other aspects of life in the Gippsland countryside also appealed and Kathy had said that she could get a transfer to the Community Hospital in town.

Still, I knew I would turn my back on all this. Terry hadn't said what he was offering but farmers are infamous for not paying well. I'd heard stories of those who would rather pay you in sides of beef or trays of eggs than shell out cash. I wanted a bank account full of money, not a room full of tucker, and I was never going to be affluent in South East Victoria.

About 10 of us set off from Gippsland to Melbourne the next morning in time to watch the Boxing Day Test Match at Melbourne Cricket Ground (MCG). It was the Third Test in the Ashes series. England had lost the first two, suffering a nine-wicket slaughter in Perth, so we desperately needed to get a win under our belt.

Although I'd grown up a stone's throw from the Oval cricket ground in London and watched a few games there, I'd never experienced anything like this. At the Oval we would politely applaud a good stroke or nice cover drive and if a fine catch caused so much as a ripple of excitement it was quickly brought under control. But Bay 13 at the MCG was an asylum. I'd never been at a Test Match where the sheer volume of noise almost prevented conversation.

On that day Dennis Lillie and Jeff Thompson didn't give us Poms much to cheer about. We later took some consolation from the Test ending in a draw but Australia won the series quite comfortably. It had been a good couple of days and I remember thinking as I took the tram down Punt Road to St. Kilda that I could get used to this life. So why was I running away again from everything I loved?

We spent New Year's Eve at the nurses' quarters in East

Melbourne and as 1975 dawned over Melbourne I walked to work feeling very pleased with myself. Kathy and I continued as if there was no threat of me ever leaving the country. We returned to Gippsland every weekend and it was life as normal.

Then, just when I was growing a little impatient and feeling a little too comfortable, I found a letter waiting for me. It said the results of my medical were fine and that I was pencilled in to leave for New Guinea on February 14— Valentine's Day.

'You can be my Valentine's present when you come back next year,' Kathy joked, trying not to show how much the news of my imminent departure upset her. We went back to the farm on the weekend before I was scheduled to leave, and an amusing thing happened.

Kathy's brother, apart from running the family business, also ran Won Wron, a local football team. The difference between this Aussie Rules team and any other was that Won Wron was an open prison.

'I get some good players every now and then, but it's hard keeping them as most don't want to hang around after they've done their time.' Terry explained, sounding disappointed.

'The nerve; no consideration some people.'

He looked at me not sure if I was making fun of him or not.

'You play a bit don't you? 'D'you wanna turn out for us tomorrow? We're having a friendly against Sale and I'm missing a full forward who was sent back to Pentridge and a ruckman who's playing truant.'

'I'll play in the ruck for you.'

I turned out for Won Wron looking not even slightly out of place. The Sale squad was so convinced I was a hardened criminal that no one came anywhere near me. I kicked six goals, won almost every bounce up and every throw in, and took over 40 possessions. In short I played my best ever game of Aussie Rules.

Terry was very impressed. 'Are you going to be available for us this season?' he asked. Kathy obviously hadn't told him.

'Sorry mate, I'm off to Bougainville next week.'

He thought that I was joking. 'No, really?'

'No, really.' Kathy confirmed.

That night we returned to the farm and Kathy finally broke it to everyone that I was going to New Guinea. The news was received in shocked silence. Why was I going? I couldn't explain to them that there was a lot of life out there for me to experience, and that this, the farm and Kathy, had been a wonderful interlude.

We returned to St Kilda on the Sunday evening. I spent the next day with Kathy and a couple of her friends who gave me a hand to clean my flat so I could reclaim my deposit. By four o'clock the place was gleaming like a new pin and when I was handed my hundred dollar bond back I gave it to the three nurses.

I had all my worldly possessions packed in a worn suitcase and toolbox. I gave Kathy the things I'd bought for the flat that I couldn't carry and at about eight o'clock we drove to the northern end of the city to book into a hotel.

There was just one more thing to do. I drove the Charger back into the city and parked it outside a well-known finance company office in Collins Street. The Charger and I had covered over 40,000 kilometres, from Perth to Port Hedland and all over the Pilbara, across the Nullarbor to Adelaide and Melbourne and then up to Sydney and Canberra.

Now I was off to New Guinea I couldn't take the Charger with me. The salesman in Perth had been right when he told me I didn't need money in this country to buy a car. I hadn't paid a penny for it, having given my address as the hostel I'd left 17 months before. I put the keys in an envelope with a short note saying thanks very much, and Kathy and I walked back to the hotel.

27

Goodbye again

I hate airport goodbyes, so Kathy and I parted at the hotel. We had an early breakfast in bed, exchanging few words as I dressed, kissed her one last time, and left her crying in the room. 'If I'd never loved I'd never have cried,' I thought to myself, eyes brimming, as I closed the door.

I walked through the hotel with a heavy heart. I'd parted from Elaine in very similar circumstances, and if I'd known Kathy for a little longer, I might never have left her. But I was on a mission, with many things I wanted to do, and places I wanted to visit. I felt certain a lot of episodes would end like this. One day I wouldn't walk away: one day I might be the one left behind in a hotel room.

Out in the street I looked up to the hotel window and returned the kiss Kathy blew to me before I reluctantly turned away. I walked the short distance to the bus terminal on King Street where the bus took me to Tullamarine Airport. As the plane climbed over the city, I made myself a promise to return. I'd enjoyed the place and I'd really enjoyed Kathy, but for now a new adventure beckoned.

As we descended into Brisbane, I caught my first glimpse of the Pacific Ocean. I'd only ever seen it in books, on television and in the movies. I was now almost as far from London as I could ever get, and I was excited at what lay ahead.

After Brisbane the flight up the coast of Queensland and across to Papua New Guinea (PNG) was uneventful. I spent as much time as I could gazing down at the varying shades of blue patchwork offered by the Pacific Ocean, with its deep water, aqua shallows and reefs. It was spectacular and I made another promise to myself to see as much of it as I possibly could.

We arrived in Port Moresby's Jackson Field Airport at one o'clock in the afternoon. The tropical heat hit me like a hammer the second I left the air-conditioned comfort of the plane. I thought I'd become used to such temperatures during my time in Port Hedland, but this heat enfolded me like a very heavy moist overcoat, leaving me dripping wet in just a few minutes.

It was a long hot wait in the customs and immigration hall where most of the fans weren't working. New Guinea was getting ready for independence after being a protectorate of Australia for many years and its self-important customs officers showed a sadistic delight in taking ages to inspect passports, visas and work permits as we melted.

From the crowded arrivals hall a group of about a dozen of us eventually found our way to the Bougainville counter in the Domestic Terminal. We were an odd assortment of black and white, young and old, male and female and as we waited in the sauna-like conditions we slowly gravitated into our own smaller groups.

The first person I met was Peter from Tasmania.

'I'm Peter,' he shook hands, 'but call me Tazzy.'

'Larry. You can call me Larry.'

We were soon joined in the queue at the counter by Chris from Broken Hill and Graham from Melbourne. As we chatted I was surprised to see a couple of nuns in the group, which made me wonder where I was going. Once we were all processed, our luggage taken and our boarding passes issued, we headed for the air-conditioned sanctuary of the lounge and more importantly to the Balus Bar. Even the nuns found relief from the heat in there.

I sat at the bar and ordered an SP stubby. Chris from Broken Hill joined me, and soon the four of us lads were enjoying a pleasant lunchtime drink.

'Cheers, here's to an enjoyable and lucrative 12 months.' Tazzy toasted.

'Cheers.' We replied. We were in the bar long enough to enjoy four or five beers before our flight was called.

I'd never flown in a small aircraft before that day so I was happy when I found myself right down the front behind the pilot, in the Cessna Caravan. I sat there listening enthralled to the chatter with the control tower as we took off for the island of Bougainville.

We weren't flying for very long before I needed to pee. I wasn't even sure that there was a toilet on the tiny plane but I spotted towards the rear a small louvered door that looked promising.

'Does this plane have a toilet?' I asked the pilot, praying that it did.

He nodded and pointed to the door I'd seen. I thanked him and made my way to the back of the plane. The cabin was so small and the ceiling so low that by the time I approached the tail of the plane I was bent in half—quite a predicament when it came to reaching the toilet bowl.

I decided I would have to sit, which meant retreating all the way back to my seat, reversing and coming in backwards. By now the focal point of the entire plane, I reached my seat, turned around and then backed down the plane. The toilet door opened outwards but I found that every time I succeeded in opening it, the door closed before I could get into the cubicle.

I was starting to sweat: I needed to go quite badly now,

and this could be really embarrassing. On my third attempt I managed to hold the door ajar just long enough to get in. closing it, I pulled down my jeans—another very tight manoeuvre since the tiny space didn't allow much movement for someone my size. To my horror, as I sat down, my knees pushed open the door again and it swung out of my reach. I sat there looking at a very perplexed but amused nun.

'How you going?' I asked to cover my embarrassment

I thought that no matter how far it was to Bougainville I wasn't doing this again. The nun obligingly closed the door for me but when I came to get dressed it was far from easy. The plane seemed to be bouncing all over the sky, rolling and lurching among ominous dark thunder clouds. I had no seat belt on and needed to return to my seat as quickly as I could.

I now ended up on the floor in the aisle with my jeans still at half-mast and only my boxer shorts saving me and the nun from total embarrassment. Fortunately the turbulence stopped as quickly as it started, allowing me to struggle back to my seat, fasten my seat belt and zip up my fly. The pilot and I exchanged a wry smile. 'You found it then?'

28

Loloho

We flew into Aropa airfield late that afternoon and I'll never forget my first feel of Bougainville. The afternoon rain had cooled the place a little but now, as the sun reappeared, the steam rose from the runway and the lush vegetation surrounding us. There was a smell I found attractive too—a smell that I have associated with the jungle ever since.

As we passed through the small terminal I exchanged a parting smile with the nun who had helped me in my moment of need. Slowly the nuns and the other passengers departed, leaving just the four of us.

A truck turned up, a man-haul. This'll do me, I thought as I threw my stuff into the back and climbed up into the truck. I pulled Graham up and in a couple of minutes we were on our way; but already Tazzy was making negative noises.

'A man-haul! This is not good enough. Who do they think we are?' he complained.

'Enjoy it Taz,' I said, ignoring him as he continued his complaining.

I hung out the back of the truck for the short trip along the beach. I had never seen black sand before, never seen palm trees growing parallel to the horizon and never seen a tropical island. I wanted to absorb everything.

The sun was sinking behind the hills around us and clouds shrouded the distant mountain tops. The jungle closed in on us making it almost dark, until suddenly we found ourselves in the small port town of Kieta where a ship out of Liverpool was unloading.

Next we turned inland, grinding down through the gears as we climbed up a hill behind Kieta. We drove away from the beach for a few minutes and passed a small village where excited children ran out to wave at us. Then the jungle closed in again and we eventually returned to the coast. It was a gorgeous drive, one I enjoyed immensely.

We eventually arrived in Arawa, a name I recognised from the magazine the company had sent me. The town had been built to accommodate a lot of the workforce from the mine, including the bulk of the married people.

We slowly drove through the town, passing the shopping centre and a sports field with a game of football in progress. Our truck stopped at an intersection on the outskirts of the town, where we turned right, returned to the beach and drove around a perfect harbour before arriving at our final destination for the day, Loloho, Camp Six.

'It's a disgrace ...' Taz went on complaining. He hadn't stopped since we arrived, but fortunately I never heard a word. I unloaded my gear and reported to the camp office where a person responsible for staff was waiting for us.

'Larry and Chris, you two have room S17.'

'Shared accommodation?' Tazzy's complaints continued.

Chris and I left him to it. We found S17 and threw our bags into the room. I wanted to go down to the wet mess to absorb a little bit more.

'Coming down to the bar Chris?' I asked, but Chris seemed a bit depressed.

'What's wrong, leave someone special behind?'

'If you don't mind I'd just rather be alone for a few minutes.'

'In here? You want to be left alone in this depressing little box? Come on, come and enjoy your new home,' I urged.

'I'll be along in a minute,' he said finally and I left him in his funk.

On my way to the wet mess I saw Graham, who was obviously in the same mood as me.

'Going for a beer?' he asked.

'Absolutely. Where's your roommate?'

'Booking a ticket home.'

'Seriously?'

'Seriously.'

'Well thank the lord for that.'

It was a beautiful night, with the last of the day fading behind us and a new moon rising over the ocean. In this romantic setting I would have loved to have traded Graham for Kathy or Elaine, just as Graham would have no doubt preferred female company to me. The wet mess was a thatched hut on the beach dispensing jugs of SP Lager. Benches were scattered across the sand, surrounded by palm trees and the sea was lapping just a few feet away.

'This'll do me mate,' I said as I poured two beers and raised my glass.

'All the best,' Graham said.

'I think it just might be,' I agreed.

29

My dad the mechanic

—&0C3—

My dad was keen on cars, but like a lot of his generation, he didn't pass his driving test until later in life. He was 35 years old before he owned his first car. Until then he had ferried the family around on a 500cc BSA motor bike and sidecar.

Dad rode the bike while my mum sat in the front of the sidecar with my sister Dena on her lap, and I sat in the tiny seat in the back of the sidecar. As we grew up, I graduated to sitting behind my dad on the bike, while Dena claimed my old seat in the back of the sidecar. We loved it. My cousin Jill who was a few years older than me thought we were the coolest, but I'm not sure my mum agreed.

Dad's first car, a black 1954 Ford Popular, broke down frequently. I would lie in bed in the morning listening to him trying to start the engine. If it didn't start straight away or after a couple of attempts, the battery quickly drained and my dad, not known for his patience, would start to lose his temper. He would resort to the starting handle but soon tired of that, and my sister and I knew what was coming next.

We never volunteered to help, preferring to stay in bed in the warm in the hope that the engine would start eventually. It never did.

'Laurence, Dena.' He would shout from the bottom of the stairs. That was all he needed to say. We knew the drill.

'Oh god.'

It was usually dark and cold out there. The car rarely misbehaved in the summer.

The three of us would heave the Ford Pop down our street towards the slight hill in Berwick Road. Sometimes a neighbour or paperboy would give us a hand and we'd push the car as far up the hill as we could until the weight stalled us.

'Ok,' Dad would announce. He'd open the door and jump in and then we would push the car down the hill as he let out the clutch. Sometimes the engine would burst into life, and he'd wave goodbye, but more often than not, the first attempt proved to be a practice run.

After the Ford Pop, he graduated to an Austin A40, then a Vauxhall Victor. He did all his own maintenance, and I think the reason I don't enjoy working on cars is because my memories of car repairs in England are all very depressing.

Without a garage, the work had to be done on the street—always in the cold and the rain—and we skinned our knuckles regularly trying to use tools that weren't up to the job. Since my dad could rarely afford the right spare part, he inevitably bought from a wreckers' yard something only marginally better than the part being replaced. No wonder we seemed to do the same job quite frequently.

Years later, after my dad retired, he moved down to the south coast, where he worked part time for a wealthy business man who owned a Jaguar. This bloke, a season ticket holder at Southampton Football Club, would take dad to a match there a couple of times a season. I remember on one of my visits home, Southampton were playing Spurs who had recently signed Villa and Ardiles from Argentina, and had put quite a useful team together. So when I saw Dad on the Sunday I asked him about the game. He had no recollection of it at all. All he remembered was the ride in the Jag.

'What a car,' he said vacantly.

Right after the house nameplate, I would love to have bought him a Jag of his own.

30

Bougainville

Despite a heavy night, we were all up and in the mess before six o'clock and for reasons unexplained I had no hangover. The island was so exhilarating and vibrant that it gave me a high. Rain had fallen during the night and I liked the smell of the wet jungle that seeped into my room. You didn't get this in London.

After breakfast we took the bus up the hill to Panguna. Of the seven in our group two had already decided that PNG wasn't for them. Apparently almost every plane load brought at least one or two who found the first night away from loved ones far too difficult to bear. I often wondered how they were received when they marched back through the door 48 hours after saying their long goodbyes. For me, it would have been harder to go back than to stay.

As soon as we turned inland on our journey to the mine site we started to climb. It was a beautiful clear morning and I wished I'd brought my camera with me as I spotted the live, smouldering volcano of Mount Bagana in the distance.

We climbed for about three quarters of an hour, rolled

over the top of the mountain range, and then eased our way into the valley below. The first sight of the pit silenced all of us. We had all worked in other mines but none as big as this one. The company had only been mining here for two years and were still commissioning, yet already the hole in the ground rivalled many of the pit's older competitors.

We were taken to the admin offices known as the Pink Palace where we met up with John Davidson and his team. A busy morning was then spent filling out reams of paperwork, having our photographs taken, bank details checked and personal details logged.

We were finally allocated rooms. I found I was sharing with Chris who I was quite happy to have as a roommate. I wasn't sure what he thought about me but he smiled amiably when he found out.

We were driven up to Camp One, passing through the small Panguna township. It resembled something from the Klondike Gold Rush or the Wild West: only the horses were missing. The wooden shacks that lined the muddy streets, with a barber's shop, travel agents even a bank, must have been photographed a thousand times. I loved the frontier feel about the place and if early impressions were anything to go by I was going to love working here.

After lunch we sat outside the mess waiting to be picked up and taken to our new workplaces. Chris went off with a friend from Broken Hill, Peter joined someone he knew and Graham and I went on waiting. I watched the clouds move through the valley below thinking I'd never lived above the clouds before.

Eventually an F100 ground its way up the hill and into the car park and a rather large gentleman squeezed himself out from behind the wheel.

'I'm looking for Larry Garner.'

'You've found him.'

Bidding goodbye to Graham I threw my toolbox into the back of the truck and Happy Frank took me to the Crusher.

He was called Happy Frank because he wasn't. Apart from Tazzy he was the first negative person I'd met since arriving on this island paradise but all his moaning went in one ear and out of the other. Fortunately when I arrived at the crusher workshop I was handed over to Sebby.

Sebby was everything Frank wasn't—a small energetic man who moved at 100 miles an hour. He came from Hamburg and inside a few minutes I found out he had been in U Boats during the war.

Before I could ask any more questions I was introduced to John Bradford, my new foreman. John was in his mid-thirties, came from Cobar, and I liked him immediately. Our chat was a formality, about what he expected from his crews and what he didn't. These days inductions take one or two days, whereas this one was over in five minutes.

'Now I have a couple of vacancies,' John told me. 'I can put you with Frank ....'

'What about Seb?' I asked, interrupting his thinking.

'Seb? Sebby's a German I thought you might want ....'

'Seb, I think, will be fine.'

'Well that's good. Seb is crushers and screens and I see you have a lot of experience in that area.'

Ten minutes later I started working in the screen house. Seb took me up to the screen floor where his crew was working, introducing me to Andy, 'Rommel', RV, and a host a Bougainvilleans. They were doing a screen change, something I hadn't done in a couple of months, but well within my scope.

The afternoon flew by and at about five I was asked if I wanted to work overtime. Of course I did: that's what I was there for. So Rommel, Andy, RV and I went back to camp to eat, then returned and stripped a crusher.

Bougainville was one of the biggest mines in the world, with a target of 100,000 tons a shift. We were still a way short of that figure but heading in the right direction. Two massive primary cone crushers fed a coarse ore stock pile, and all we concentrated on was making small rocks out of big ones.

I spent that first evening in the crusher working with a bunch of guys who, though I didn't know it at the time, were going to become my best mates. Nearly 40 years later I am still friends with most of them.

I found out most of these guys were fairly new to Bougainville too and we all tried to present a can-do attitude so the job went well. A little after midnight we took our tags off, waited back until the machine started up, and headed back to Camp One. Although it was late Rommel, Andy and I sat out on the steps behind our rooms enjoying a drink. The beer never tasted better.

'Now Larry, we've worked over 17 hours today,' Rommel began. 'If you make sure you show up tomorrow at seven you'll be paid double time all day.'

I thought he was winding me up but Andy, a more sober character than Rommel, convinced me it was true.

'The "magic 17" they call it,' he told me. 'Work over 17 hours and you get paid double time the next day if you come in on schedule.'

My watch said it was ten past one. I was tired but in excellent company and the steps by our rooms became our social club after many a night's work.

We seemed to be able to work as long as we wanted, starting at seven and putting in 16, 17 or 18 hours—even an occasional 24-hour shift. Whenever our stint was round the clock we went to bed straight after breakfast, but were usually called in that same night. For most of my time there life seemed to be all work and no play.

Every now and then we would have a day off, just because we were so exhausted. One night after I had worked 36 days straight, averaging 14 hours a day, I was with Seb, Rommel and 'Burgess' as Andy was becoming more frequently called. We had a few beers on the steps and talked ourselves into having the next day off. We were looking forward to the break.

31

A strange coincidence

The next morning after breakfast we caught the night shift bus down to the coast making for Pub Island. We first stopped at Arawa, the main town on the coast, to do a few errands. Like most blokes, I don't like shopping, but once in a while it's nice to buy something you really need like soap, or in my case a cassette player and half a dozen cassettes. As I was seriously thinking about staying in Bougainville for a while I decided a bit of music would help to make me comfortable.

We needed transport too, as became obvious when we wanted to continue to the town of Kieta. With a poor bus service and taxis few and far between we started walking but Seb, who must have been in his 60s, soon tired of that so we eventually waved down a passing taxi to take us the six kilometres to Kieta.

The town had been the working port of Bougainville long before the mine was even thought of, since the turn of the century in fact. The same was true of the Chinese general store that sold everything from anchors to ice. What an interesting place—I could have spent the day in there. After visiting the general store we headed up the street to the Kieta Hotel.

It was hot down on the coast. Living up in Panguna we weren't used to the heat and it didn't take long to feel the bite of the sun. Even before lunchtime it was sweltering out there.

Burgess had worked for the company during the construction of the mine. He told us they had built a resort just out from Kieta on Aropa Island, now commonly known as Pub Island.

The ferry to the island left from the Kieta Hotel so, while Burgess and Seb went looking for the ferry master, Rommel and I bought the beers. What a location it was, right down on the water with a splendid view out over the South Pacific. Rommel and I sat at a table on deck. If we had sat there all day I would have been quite happy.

When Burgess and Seb returned after a few they announced that, sitting on deck where we were, might be as close as we were going to get to Pub Island.

'The engine has thrown a bearing,' Seb told us. 'They're waiting for parts from Moresby.' He said the ferry might be ready in a couple of days, but it wouldn't be running out to the island today.

'No other boats?' Rommel asked.

'Don't know, didn't ask.'

'I could live here,' I said, gazing out over the ocean.

'You've only been here five minutes,' Seb said.

'I could buy a boat, run charters and sail around the islands. I could work up at the mine during shutdowns and spend the rest of my time down here on the water.'

'You'd be bored out of your mind in no time,' said Burgess.

'No, no I wouldn't. There are a million things to do when you have a boat like fishing, diving, maintenance, women ... I wouldn't find time to get bored.'

No-one offered any more arguments.

'Might join you ...' Rommel conceded.

We spent an hour in the pub, enjoyed a good lunch, and just when we seemed to be settling in for the afternoon, Burgess suggested a walk along the esplanade.

There were all sorts of craft moored along the quay, including a couple of yachts, a small coaster and the Meadowbank, the big ship from Liverpool that was docked here the day I arrived.

'I wonder if we can go aboard,' I said absently as we approached the ship and noticed a bit of life.

'Any chance of a look around?' Seb asked a guy coming down the gang plank.

'Shouldn't be a problem. Wait here, I'll be back in a minute after I've just mailed these letters and I'll take you aboard myself,' he said in a very cut glass English accent.

When he returned he gave us a quick tour of the ship. I had always entertained ideas of going to sea when I was growing up. I thought romantic thoughts of travelling to the South Seas but my dad told me that most of the people who went to sea were 'a sad bunch of drunks'. Our guide gave no indication at all that he was sad or drunk.

We ended up in the galley where we met the first mate, chief engineer and purser, and when it became known that there were guests aboard, the skipper joined us. I feared they might have thought us intrusive or just downright nosey for almost inviting ourselves aboard, but apparently it was not unusual in foreign ports and we were made quite welcome. The skipper, Les Toogood from Liverpool, was an older man, probably the same vintage as Seb.

'Have you been at sea all of your life?' I asked.

'Not yet,' came his well-used reply. We politely laughed.

'I've been at sea nearly 40 years, most of it with the Bank Line, but I did a few years with the Blue Flu and the Blue Funnel.'

As he filled his pipe and the beers were passed around Les continued, 'I joined up as a cadet in 1937 and sailed the North Atlantic run from New York to Liverpool and back.'

'Did you ever run up to Archangel and Murmansk?' I asked.

He nodded. 'During the war, we were seriously damaged on one of our runs up there.'

He was good at telling stories and we warmed to him as he set the scene.

'One bitterly cold afternoon in late November it was getting dark although it was only about three o'clock. I was on watch looking for U Boats, but visibility was too poor to see any tell-tale tales signs. All of a sudden, without warning, a tanker way off our port beam erupted. We saw just a massive flash at first and then the boom reached us a few seconds later.

'The tanker only burned for a couple of minutes before she went down: there would have been no survivors. Less than 10 minutes later another tanker off our port beam, closer than the first, was hit by one torpedo and then a second. We were about to manoeuvre to pick up survivors but our escort told us to maintain course. If you slowed down, they believed, you became an easier target.

'The skipper wasn't keen on leaving possible survivors behind and he was seriously considering ignoring the order when we were hit ourselves. It felt like the whole ship leapt out of the water.'

'What were you carrying?' I asked.

'We were a refrigerator/freezer ship carrying frozen food. The first torpedo blew our engine room to bits and everyone in there: the second tore a hole in our bow so that we immediately started to take on water and list.'

'Were you on the Empire Glade?' Seb asked.

There was a stone cold silence as the two men looked at each other. Les had never mentioned the name of the ship so there was only one way Seb could have known.

'You sank us?' Les asked.

'I think so. The tanker was an American ship, the Hector Valley, and the ship we hit before yours was ....'

'... our sister ship the Empire Lea. My brother went down with that ship.'

The silence lingered. 'I'm sorry,' Seb said finally. 'Would you like me to leave?'

'No, no. All of this happened a long time ago and it's about time it was put to bed.' He was really very casual about it.

'Tell us about your war Seb. Were you ever sunk?' Les asked.

'Oh yes.' He described the terror of sitting at his station listening to the depth charges exploding all around and wondering if the next one might just be the one to hit their U Boat.

'But we were on the surface charging our batteries when our boat was sunk. We were in the Sargasso Sea, not far from Bermuda, on a beautiful afternoon and I was on watch with two others taking in the sunshine when we were hit by dive bombers. Two direct strikes blew the boat into the next century and blew me about a hundred metres.' Seb's German accent was perfect for his story.

'We survived in the water for three days and three nights. Sharks came close on a few occasions but fortunately never touched us. We were in the shipping lanes and a U Boat supply ship eventually picked us up and brought us back to Bremen.

'When I next went to sea we were sunk again. It was a year later in the Mediterranean and depth charges hit us. We managed to reach the surface where we fought a gun battle with a destroyer. We came second, but luckily managed to avoid capture because they shot at us in the water and left us for dead .... Not very pleasant times, Les.'

'You're right.'

'Whose gonna top that?' Burgess asked looking at Rommel and me.

We could both tell a fairly good story, but Les and Seb were in a different class.

Our time aboard came to an end as our sailor friends had to sail with the afternoon tide, so we thanked them for their hospitality and wished them good luck. We waved as they slipped their moorings, promising them a tour of the mine and plant next time around, but I never saw Les again.

We headed back up the hill to Panguna. My little adventure seemed to pale compared to Seb's. Back in my room with the light out, I thought of Seb listening to the depth charges and wondering if the next charge would end it all. No, I thought, Seb could have his adventure. I was quite happy with mine.

32

Squash

After that first day off, I decided that if I was going to stay and do a year here I might need a regular break. Working 24/7 was all well and good for the bank account, but I needed to enjoy life a bit or I might burn out. So I got talking with the guys and Toby suggested I join the squash club.

'Competition night is every Wednesday night. It's a lot of fun.'

'I've never played.' I told him.

'It's simple. What could be easier that slamming a ball against a wall?'

'What indeed.'

They had four grades at the Panguna Squash Club starting with the grade A players who were the elite, down to those in grade D who really hadn't quite mastered the finesse of the game. I started in D grade and showed all the subtle skills that D-graders brought to the game.

They had four courts, one glass-backed so that the dedicated followers of squash could watch while having a drink. The squash club was also a very lively social club so I did what I did best—I socialised. By the time I was up to play I was far too inebriated to play a proper game, let alone win one.

A massive invisible wall separated the married men and the single men. Single, expat guys were without doubt the lowest form of life anywhere on the island. We were rarely or never invited to parties. Only Ditchy and JD invited us sorry single blokes to theirs, but even then they often regretted it. The women were out of bounds so we concentrated on getting drunk, fighting and making complete idiots of ourselves.

At least at the squash club we could actually talk to a member of the opposite sex which was quite refreshing. There were about 50 women members, mainly the wives of the guys I worked with. Usually the woman's husband was right beside her with a very tight grip on her leash, but it was better than nothing. I played against some women who made us feel welcome like the lovely Anna Santorini, or Anna Santorinickers as I called her because she had a penchant for wearing little frilly knickers under her ultra mini, and I loved her for it.

There were also the friendly PNG women who played, two of whom had married my best mates. Rommel married Oven, an air hostess from Rabaul while Harvey married Joslynn, a lass from Buka. Both women were smashing, but those who knew them were certain which of our mates got the best of the deal. Oven was by far the prettiest and smartest in her family, and Harvey must have thanked his lucky stars every night he went to bed.

Thinking about the squash club conjures up these thoughts. It was supposed to be a sports club but it meant different things to different people. Unfortunately I only played squash there.

After losing my first two games, I started to take squash seriously and crept up the ladder until I found my true level at the higher end of grade C. Toby on the other hand became not only our club champion, but also went on to play overseas, representing Bougainville in places like Rabaul and Honiara.

I remember a famous exchange a few years later when club members were talking about Toby's exploits.

'Rabaul's not overseas,' someone said, trying to downplay what Toby had achieved.

'You ever driven there?' I asked.

33

Have bike will travel

We continued to work whatever hours were available, nearly always doing double shifts on Tuesdays when we dealt with Line One shutdowns, and on Thursdays when we covered Line Two. I usually tried to make Wednesday a 10-hour shift in order to get the evening off, and would just see what came along on the other days.

In 1975 I earned $2.75 an hour, and for what was considered a regular week we would gross $257.50.

We were paid fortnightly and during one two-week period I grossed over a $1,000 with overtime. Rommel and Burgess were regularly doing the same.

When you work shifts totalling well over 100 hours a week as we did, sleep comes automatically after a few beers, and almost everything else is forgotten.

I never shaved or had a haircut for a year—not much point as there were no women to impress. The squash court was my sole contact with the opposite sex, and a glimpse of Anna Santorini's knickers my only consolation.

After working until about seven one night, I returned

to the camp, had a shower and dived head first into bed. At about nine thirty Old Mick knocked on my door. He took one look at me and said, 'You look just like Harpo Marx.' And for the rest of my life I have been Harpo, the tall Pommy bastard with the beard. Thanks Mick.

Our little group wasn't complete until two new boilermakers, Uncle Ron and Bagdad Bill, turned up right out of the blue. As soon as they arrived I liked 'em. Both could work hard and enjoyed a drink. Ron came from Newcastle, and Bagdad was from Beirut via Sydney. Bagdad was the first Muslim I ever got to know, although I don't think he was practicing because he liked a beer a bit too much. What Ron and Bagdad both brought to our little circle was a passion for motorbikes. Ron had a 360 DT Yamaha shipped to the site, and as soon as we saw him riding it we knew we had to have bikes too.

My quest was to save money, but I reasoned with myself that I would save more if I managed to spend $1,000 on a motorbike. It made sense then, and in hindsight it was indeed a sound investment. The next week Ela Motors sold four 250 Suzukis to four hairy-arsed tradesmen. I bought one, as did Rommel, Bagdad Bill and Toby, while Burgess bought a 1944 Willy's Jeep. In less than a week we were mobile.

When I was a Mod in London during the swinging 60s I had briefly ridden a scooter, a green Vespa GS 160 with copper bubbles and Cadillac crash bars. I paid a fiver for it and I was ripped off. Now I had a real motorbike, and Uncle Ron showed me how to ride it. He treated every hill as a challenge and I lost more skin learning to ride that thing than in any other adventure.

We headed for the Jabba river near the mine. The land down there was like the surface of the moon, a vast area that had been cleared and an ideal place to put a bike through its paces. We had a lot of fun—I still wear the scars, and I wasn't the only one who needed patching up. Luckily, I happened to be taking my St John's Ambulance certificate at the time.

34

Traces of war

Bougainville was in the middle of the war in the South Pacific and the Battle of Guadalcanal was fought next door between the Allied forces and Japan. Chief of the Japanese operations in the South Pacific, Isoruku Yamamoto, was shot down over Bougainville and crashed near the town of Buin. Apparently there was a lot to see in the south of the island, so seven of us decided that a weekend off was long overdue and that we would take a trip to Buin.

Uncle Ron, Bagdad, Rommel, Graham and I travelled by motorbike, while Burgess drove the supply jeep with Thomas Mele riding shotgun. Thomas, who was Rommel's apprentice, came from Buin and knew how to get there which we all figured was kind of important.

In the short time I'd worked on Bougainville I'd got to know half a dozen of the local lads quite well, and slowly a friendship was developing. My offside, James Tullumby, wanted to come with us too but he was unsure as to how he would be received down in Buin, so the day before we left he declined the invitation.

We understood his reasoning. PNG is a country of simple rules. If someone from your village once hit someone from my village it's only fair that I'll hit you. Pay-back in New Guinea where the people have long memories is very real. James was a Tolai from Rabaul and if a Tolai had ever upset anyone down in Buin poor old James might have had a sticky old weekend.

We left on the Saturday morning in excellent weather. It would rain later—you could set your watch by the four o'clock downpour—but we were prepared for all eventualities. As we weren't sure if there would be petrol down there or how much they would charge us for it, the jeep was loaded with two jerry cans of fuel. We were going to be away overnight so we each brought a couple of barbecue packs from the mess.

We filled one esky with a couple of cartons of beer and another with tucker. I think I was the only one who actually packed a change of clothes. We were going bush, real bush. Still, you just never knew what might be around the corner!

We left at eight and headed down to the coast, but before reaching Arawa we turned south along a dirt trail and after a few minutes had to negotiate our first river crossing. In those days I was very patriotic so I claimed the crossing for the Queen and sprayed a rock pink in the same way that the British Commonwealth is always depicted in pink on most maps. I called the place Harpo's Crossing, a name it still bears to this day—one of my few claims to fame.

It's about 85 miles to Buin and we averaged about 15 miles an hour. The bikes could have eaten it up but the jeep, although quite useful on the bitumen, was long retired from the kind of four-wheel driving that parts of the road demanded. There were many river crossings with many opportunities to have a soak while we waited.

By about mid-day, when we had covered over half the distance, we found an excellent river that was shallow enough to cross but also deep enough for a swim. Burgess jumped out of the jeep, toilet roll in hand, and headed into the jungle.

Busy with the barbecue, we had forgotten about him until someone asked about the couple of snags that were beginning to turn to charcoal on the plate. We were about to go looking for him when he emerged from the bush.

'You'll never believe what I've just found.' he said. We shook our heads. 'Come with me.'

We walked deep into the bush for about five minutes then there it was—an American fighter plane, a Corsair that had obviously been shot down. Unbelievably the burnt out cockpit still smelled of smoke. The rest of the plane was in good condition with its wings and guns intact, which suggested not too many people had stumbled across the plane and stripped it of souvenirs.

As we took some photos, I wondered if the pilot got out or whether he was incinerated in this spot. I thought of spraying a part of the wreck pink and claiming it for the Queen, but better judgement prevailed.

An hour further down the road Thomas told us that we were approaching the Yamamoto shrine. He didn't mention that this was where the track to it started. We set off into the dense jungle expecting a similar five minute walk into the scrub to the one we'd just done, but it was an hour before we finally arrived at a simple monument that had been erected in memory of General Yamamoto.

The worn track indicated that this spot was frequently visited. Yamamoto's body had been returned to Japan and his Betty Bomber, in similar condition to the Corsair, was still identifiable. Again we were silenced by what we saw. Although in this crowd a joke was never far away, we all felt, as with the Corsair, that joking here would be inappropriate.

I felt quite pleased with myself. Many, many people had worked on Bougainville and many knew about Yamamoto's shrine but few had actually seen it. I'm ashamed to say I got my spray can out and marked the Betty, not to claim it for the Queen, just to prove to others that I had been there.

At about four in the afternoon we finally arrived in Buin,

a town which, in the years leading up to independence, had
served as a local administration centre. A few expats still
worked there, although what they did was anybody's guess.
The town's Colonial Club, run nowadays by Australia, still
bore all the trappings of a British colonial club with all its
stupid rules.

We obviously weren't members but you would have
thought that they would have welcomed some fresh company,
not to mention some dollars over the bar. However they were
typical of a number of colonialists I've met—narrow-minded,
petty little people who jealously flaunted their membership of
an organisation that no one outside their little clique could
care less about. I was disappointed but not surprised, and we
left them for much better company.

We travelled a few miles down the road to Thomas's
village where, as friends of one of the sons of the community,
we were received like Wantoks or close comrades in arms.
I would take this kind of company every time over members
of the Colonial Club.

We spent the night feasting on *cus-cus* and flying fox—
not exactly my first choice but apparently the Beef Wellington
was off. The food was what my dad would have called an
acquired taste. I did have a barbecue pack left, but I thought
you shouldn't knock this until you'd tried it.

Fish was also on the menu, which made a lot of sense
since we were almost living on the beach. I settled for the fish
and wasn't disappointed. We slept rough in sleeping bags on
the floor of Thomas's beachfront apartment.

In the morning when we went out in Thomas's outrigger
canoe and caught breakfast, I also caught a glimpse of my first
real dorsal fin as it broke the surface a few metres away, and
its tail fin about a metre behind it. I figured it was about six
foot long but Thomas was unfazed so I took it all in my stride.
We returned to find that Rommel had got a fire going and
warmed up the billy can.

After breakfast, Thomas took us along the beach to

show us Shortland Island, part of the Solomon chain, on the horizon. Any map of the region shows Bougainville is really more part of the Solomon Islands than PNG, and this is also evident from the how similar the people are. That didn't stop the white colonisers in their supreme arrogance deciding to run the dividing line, then put Bougainville in New Guinea and Shortland Island in the Solomons.

Not far from the village, about 10 minutes along the beach, we found a Japanese gun emplacement. A short tunnel system, with beds, tables and crude furniture still intact, had obviously served as the Japs' makeshift camp. There were even Saki bottles still on the table!

Years later on every Anzac Day at his place in Queensland, Rommel would serve his celebrated home brew in those Saki bottles. I think he asked Thomas to round up as many bottles as he could find and I'm sure he paid him well for his trouble.

Just behind the gun emplacement was a runway with Betty Bombers lined up on either side ready for another attack on the Allies. But the order never came and the jungle had reclaimed much of the runway. The planes were showing a few signs of age, yet I honestly believed that if we'd had the time we might have got one started: it was a wartime playground. We vowed not to tell anyone about our find because the planes could easily have been picked clean by souvenir hunters and probably were within a few years.

It took us nearly five hours to get back to Panguna. Not long after we left Buin the skies opened up, completely flooding the track. The rivers became quite fast and dangerous—so much so that the jeep got bogged twice and twice we had to drag it out of the water. We were all tired, and I'm sure everyone was as glad as I was to see Harpo's Crossing and the bitumen in the gathering gloom.

As we rode into Panguna, escorting the jeep up the hill to Camp One, the rain was falling harder than ever. I was really looking forward to a shower, a good feed and my bed, but Sebby was standing outside my room and I knew it was not to be.

'Ah Harpo, enjoy your little break?'

He didn't need to say any more. I got changed, we had a bite to eat, and then Rommel and I jumped into the truck and set off to work.

35

My dad's furniture

—∞∝—

My dad was making steel furniture long before those famous Swedish stores with their self-assembly products came along. There wasn't a lot of money in our home, but enough, and Dad would rarely buy something if he could make it.

He was a sheet metal worker by trade and we lived in a house full of his homemade creations. Book cases, beds, wardrobes, shelves, wall units, even the kitchen table and chairs ... everything was made out of sheet metal. He made things in pieces at work and somehow managed to smuggle whatever he had made over the factory wall, onto the roof rack of his motorbike and home. I was frequently asked to give him a hand bringing the stuff inside.

If it was a bed, and he had made many, he would assemble it in the room and cover it with wood grained wallpaper so that to the untrained eye it looked like the real thing. Wherever one of his pieces was placed it normally stayed in that spot. In all the years that we lived in that house my mother rarely rearranged the furniture: she'd have needed a fork lift truck.

My dad was equally adept in all the home maintenance skills. When he got a word that there was a Parkray central heating unit going cheap somewhere, he bought it. I helped him to get the unit home. There were half a dozen radiators, including one with a nasty crease across the panel, together with nameless accessories and a lot of pipes.

This was going to be a serious construction job that involved pulling out the back boiler and the fireplace and knocking around part of the chimney breast and a bit of the kitchen—nothing my dad couldn't handle. So the next morning we set about demolishing the fireplace.

As this was a rented house belonging to the local council, you weren't really supposed to make such alterations without permission, but since the council rarely let tenants do anything, my dad wasn't going to waste his time asking them.

Over three days we ran radiators to each of the three bedrooms (I was lucky enough to get the creased one) and installed three downstairs. We plumbed it all in and waited for the central heating to come on at the flick of a switch. It didn't work.

We didn't try it again at that point because we had installed the system during the summer, and we didn't really need it for the time being. A couple of months later though, I came home from school one afternoon and there was a definite chill in the air. I had learned how to start up the central heating and it seemed to come on, but it wasn't really throwing out any heat unless you sat right on top of the fire.

When Dad came home he noticed the chill.

'You got the fire on?' he asked. It obviously was on, so he went around to all the radiators and bled them. Then he opened up the back of the unit and played around with something.

'There you go,' he said, 'that's fixed.' He hadn't actually fixed anything. He never conceded he might have bought a lemon, and for the next couple of days he walked around the house in a singlet while Dene and I were wrapped up like polar bears.

'I don't know what's wrong with you two. Anyone would think that it's cold.'

He continued with this charade for another couple of days until I noticed him shivering in his T-shirt as Dene and I shivered under a blanket.

It got seriously cold a day or so later and when he cancelled the removal of the back boiler and the old grate I knew he was caving in.

'Come on,' he said conceding, 'you are going to have to give me a hand.'

We had some wonderful neighbours; Mrs O'Keefe next door was a diamond, Gwen a few doors down was a rock, as were Peggy and Arthur at the end of our block. Unfortunately, however, there was Doris.

Doris and her hen-pecked family thought they were better than the rest of us, and had a nasty habit of reporting various indiscretions to the authorities. Doris didn't like to think that any of the neighbours were getting ahead of her.

After Mr O'Keefe next door built an aviary, Doris became involved and he had to knock it down because he had no permission. Then there was Bill, Gwen's husband, who built a shed, and received a council visit. Because it was a proper shed, on a slab and looked attractive, the council gave him all the correct papers to fill in and allowed him to keep it, but the word was out that Doris was watching. And listening to us, it seemed. She must have heard some of the sledge hammer work because she reported us to the council. She couldn't bear the thought that we might be installing central heating.

Fortunately the wheels turned slowly and it was a week after Dad and I had reversed the installation that the building inspector knocked on the door. He introduced himself and told my dad who he was.

'We have reason to believe that you may have carried out an unauthorised modification to this house.'

'Really? Well you're welcome to come in and have a look.'

It took less than a minute for the inspector to see his information was incorrect.

'I'm sorry Mr Garner there seems to have been a mistake. We were told that you had installed a central heating unit.'

'Well as you can see I haven't. You can't beat a good old open fire.'

Then as he was showing the inspector out he added, 'But I do know where there's a good used Parkray unit should anyone you know be interested.'

'Really?' the inspector replied, showing a bit of interest. 'Installing a central heating unit isn't something you're not allowed to do, you just have to get permission for the change.'

'I'll remember that,' Dad told him.

Later that evening the phone rang. It was the building inspector.

'Mr Garner I'm interested in what you said about being able to put your hands on a Parkray.'

'Complete unit and six radiators—I think that's the deal.'

'How much?'

'The bloke paid 40 quid for it but I know he'll take 30.'

The next day after school I was in the back garden cleaning up the Parkray and running a rag over the radiators and other accessories. Next we loaded everything into the back of Dad's works van and he delivered it to the inspector. When my dad came home he gave me a pound. I was chuffed and so was he—he'd made 10 quid. I thought that was the last of it until the very next day when I bumped into Doris.

'We're getting central heating just like you.' She couldn't wait to tell me.

'Really?'

'Really. A Parkray.'

'I hear they're good.'

'The best,' she boasted.

When I came home from school the next day and saw a central heating unit being carried up the path to Doris' front door, I thought it looked very familiar. But it was the creased radiator that really gave it away.

—⬥—

36

The housewarming

W e had known for a while that Camp One was going to be razed because, like most of Panguna, it sat on top of a very rich ore deposit. I think the eventual aim was to move everyone down to Arawa but in the meantime Panguna was being developed into a very modern town.

We were moving into a recently built four-storey residential block and a new shopping centre was to be the hub of the town, complete with supermarket, post office, bank, travel agent, a number of variety stores and a coffee shop. The old shanty town of Panguna would soon be no more than a fond memory.

When they finally closed the old supermarket, it was a sad occasion. The last day I ever shopped there in the rain and the mud was also the last day we were allowed to ride into town in the back of a ute. Safety rules were creeping into the industry, and in future we would take a bus to do our banking and shopping. Bougainville was moving towards the twenty first century, dragging its workers kicking and screaming behind it.

I moved into C Block with Rommel as a room-mate while we waited for single accommodation. The end of Camp One was the end of an era and to celebrate moving into our new home we decided to have a cheese and wine evening. Wasn't that a good idea!?

If the management had their way they would have hired only married men whom they regarded as much more stable and easier to manipulate than the single guys. But that was never going to happen, so they tolerated us as best they could and we made our own entertainment which usually involved getting drunk, falling over and fighting.

With our social evening, however, we decided to change our image. All the usual suspects were invited to bring their favourite tipple to Harpo and Rommel's place where cheese and nibbles would be supplied by the hosts. Burgess brought some Galliano, which we all agreed made an excellent fighting bottle (although when you got in close you couldn't beat the Mateus Rosé which didn't taste too bad either).

Burgess gave everyone a glass of Galliano and proceeded to show off by setting fire to his. We all followed suit. Unfortunately, Razza tried to drink his glass while it was still burning, setting his beard alight and really doing a number on his lips and the curtains. That more or less set the trend for the night. I woke up downstairs in the laundry, completely naked, with my clothes in the tumble drier.

37

Crash

I t was becoming common for me to spend Christmas away from home, but how the married men among us survived is something I'll never understand. In the mid-1970s, with no email or mobile phones, communication was difficult at best. Telephones existed of course. Alex G Bell's invention had managed to penetrate a fair chunk of PNG and we had phones at work, but calling home was extremely difficult, especially if you didn't have the use of an office in your job.

I was single so I didn't care. I wrote to various girlfriends, but the fire had gone out of all of my romances. I knew monks who had more fun than me.

A lot of the married guys spent a large part of their evenings and their salaries in the two phone booths outside the post office. I felt for them, I really did, especially with Christmas coming up.

I had a number of friends who had left families behind and I understood why they did it. If you did a year up here you could save about 15 grand. Since a new home in the Melbourne suburbs cost about 30 grand at that time, if you did two years

you almost had the house paid off. Most of the wives left
behind understood and were extremely supportive.

Glenn, Joe and Ken received boxes from their wives
that took six weeks to arrive, full of photos and letters and
presents, and they all shared their presents with me. But for
every dozen or so good wives, there was one horror story that
none of the married men wanted to hear about.

Crash, who came from Bendigo, worked in the power
station in Loloho on the coast where we were often sent to
help with shutdowns. In the six or so months I'd worked there
I'd done a number of jobs with Crash and we made a good
team. He had sent every penny he earned home. He envied us
our jaunts on our motorbikes, and although we hardly ever
had any time off, we seemed almost part-time compared to
him.

I was with him on his last shift when he completed his
12 months' stint. We had changed the head pulley on one of
the ship loading conveyors and in the late afternoon we stood
at the end of the springboard while she started up. The rain
that had kindly held off during the installation started just
after we removed our tags, soaking us to the skin as we waited
for the sparkies to sort out electrical problems that always
dogged us at this stage. 'Home for Christmas, Crash eh? Wish
I had half your luck.'

'It'll be your turn one day Harpo,' he smiled, trying to
sweeten my pill.

'I'm not even half way.'

As soon as the conveyor eventually started up, Crash
and I walked its length checking the tracking. We waited in
the rain until they put feed on and when we were satisfied
that our part of the job was finished we started the long walk
back to the workshop. Crash, toolbox on his shoulder, was
walking down the conveyor in front of me when suddenly
without any warning he turned, threw his toolbox onto the
conveyor and—whoosh—off she went to Japan!

'Good riddance!' He said, 'I'm never using the tools

again.' I was tempted to do the same but I still needed mine. We said goodbye and I really didn't think that I would ever see him again.

But I did, a lot sooner than I ever imagined. I met him in the Coastal Club three weeks later on the weekend before Christmas.

'Crash, what the hell are you doing here?' I asked, shaking his hand.

'I knew something was wrong when she wasn't at the airport to meet me.'

'Oh shit, what happened?'

'I hired a car and drove to Bendigo to find the house had been cleaned out, as had me bank account. Twelve endless months in this place and absolutely nothing to show for it.'

I shook my head. 'I'm sorry Crash, I really am.'

'But do you know what the worst part was Harpo?'

Oh no, I hate it when a man cries, but I had to be an ear when I knew he needed one.

'No mate, what was that?'

'Buying a new fuckin' toolbox ! D'you know how much tools cost these days?'

I laughed. 'C'mon mate, I'll buy you a drink.'

৵

Christmas Day arrived in Bougainville, and what better way to celebrate the holiday than working 16 hours! I earned more than I'd ever earned before. Everyone who was married had the day off, but for us single blokes who had nobody except each other to celebrate with, it was a bonanza.

We nipped back at six for a quick bite that didn't really do justice to the work put in by the kitchen staff. They had really gone out of their way to provide a full Christmas dinner with all the trimmings, and we showed our appreciation by woofing it down in a few minutes and racing back to work.

It was almost midnight before Rommel, Burgess and

I could sit out on the steps with a couple of beers and wish each other Merry Christmas. And that was it. In my room was a small parcel from home with presents wrapped in Christmas paper from my sisters, my dad and Elaine. I loved them for their thoughtfulness. Heading across the road with a pocket full of change I tried to phone them but either the system was overloaded or just wasn't working. For a few minutes I felt really, really homesick.

38

Missed overtime

We had worked every day since coming back from Buin so some time off was overdue, but we wanted to work New Year's Day in order to be paid double time. First, however, there was the dance up at the new cricket club.

It was the usual Panguna affair with 100 hairy-arsed fitters and a dozen available women. I did manage to grab a partner for a couple of dances, but when the music slowed a hovering boyfriend or husband slipped in and I was forced to make the long walk back to the bar.

Midnight came when you shake hands with blokes you don't like and kiss women you don't know. As there was a bar extension for New Year's Eve, we stayed until the end. Then we joined a party at the home of Kiwi, one of the few married men who tolerated us single types. We partied on there for another couple of hours before heading back to the steps to finish New Year's Day just as the sun was coming up.

Work was calling. Back in those days it was a sign of your masculinity if you could work while completely legless.

In fact I've done some of my best jobs in that condition.
I returned to my room, changed for work and dashed down to breakfast.

I was sitting with Rommel, Harvey, Horny, Norm, and Jo, and I had my back to the door, when all of a sudden there was this huge commotion outside. A gang of drunken Tolai people from Rabaul burst in and ran amuck, grabbing food and throwing it back at the kitchen staff.

They overturned tables and threw the plates of startled diners across the mess, but as they approached our table I was ready for them. I smashed my plate into one guy's face—the fight back had begun.

Rommel followed suit as I knew he would, and I think someone else did too. The whole place just erupted. Someone threw a chair at me which I caught and hit another Tolai fella with it. There was a lot of shouting. Rommel went down, I kicked someone's head, and someone else struck me.

By the time security finally turned up I had one of the Tolai group around the neck and he was hit with a tray. Rommel lay on the ground with a bloke on top of him trying to bury his head in the concrete floor, and I was just about to remove his attacker's head from his shoulders when more security and the police arrived. The batons came out—the cue to make a run for it—but 10 minutes later we were all rounded up, thrown in the back of the paddy wagon and taken down to the local nick.

Rommel's nose was all over his face and there were a few others who looked equally out of sorts. Down the nick Rommel was taken to the sick bay while I was thrown into a cell and had to wait to be bailed out.

When the word spread that we were in the lock up, Harvey and Big Danny went around collecting bail money. They broke off on hearing that Rommel had been transferred to Arawa Hospital, and together with a dozen of my best friends they set off down the coast to visit him, completely forgetting about me.

They found Rommel with a badly broken nose, a split lip and a cut over his eye. When he emerged from the casualty ward he looked like he'd gone 15 rounds with Rocky, but he was warmly received and they carried their hero down to the Coastal Club where the New Year's Day celebrations continued.

It wasn't until they came back up the hill at about three o'clock that I was finally bailed out. Ironically it was Rommel who brought the bail money in.

'Thanks mate,' I said. 'Jeez, you look a picture.'

He gave me one of his looks. 'D'you know what hurts even more Harpo? We've missed out on double time and a half all day!'

Rommel wasn't the only person who had been taken to hospital that day: a total of four people were transferred for treatment. The fight had been quite a serious affair and came to the notice of not just the police, but also the management of the company. Unfortunately it was seen as a racial incident, which wasn't good. Our future hung in the balance.

I was guilty of nothing more than self-defence and most of the security people and many witnesses backed me up on that. The trouble was that what the police had seen when they came in was me thumping someone with a chair and kicking someone in the head. Luckily, apart from our bosses whose mess had been turned into a real mess and who wanted some sort of restitution, no-one was pressing charges. All we wanted to do was go back to work.

The incident never came to trial. A hearing a week or so later concluded that security staff should have headed off the threat long before we became involved, and that security arrangements had been inadequate that morning. I had more than one character witness lined up to testify that I was not a racist, and although they were never called upon, I appreciated the support.

39
The riot

The riot that followed made our little skirmish seem like a picnic. Totally unrelated to our incident it was the culmination of serious discontent that had been bubbling under the surface for a while.

After two years of operations the mine had failed to produce the returns expected, and the money the locals had been promised was going instead to Port Moresby to line the pockets of people there.

Finally, over 1000 angry local workers and their supporters went on a rampage. They smashed up the cricket club and ran through Karawong Haus where the mess, only just repaired after the New Year's Day fight, was turned over again. But it was when the protesters headed up Married Hill, the section of Panguna where most of the top brass and their families lived, that people became really concerned.

A road block was set up and the police fired tear gas to disperse the crowd. This brought only a temporary reprieve, but enough to evacuate the families. Half a dozen buses turned up to ferry the women and children to the Jaba river, which for some reason was considered safe. (In fact the first person on the bus was Big Raddy the rigger, who assured the doubtful passengers he would protect them if anything should happen during the trip.)

We stayed at work until the place was shut down. A skeleton crew was supposed to stay back with the critical equipment while the rest of us headed down to the Jaba river. We didn't go. Instead we did a scout around on the bikes to find out where the crowds were. It was exciting; not exactly Beirut, but interesting just the same.

When they broke into the cricket club the rioters stole all the beer, then retreated to Karoona Haus and set up road blocks. An uneasy peace descended while they got 'sparked up'.

We waited for the riot squad from Moresby and Lae, who were flown in that evening and trucked up to Panguna at about six o'clock the following morning. A couple of hundred riot police arrived at the police station just down the road from Karawong and we had a grandstand seat from the ledge outside my room watching them get ready.

This was meat and potatoes for them, and I felt a kind of sympathy for people like Thomas who was no doubt involved in the protest and would probably get a good kicking.

During the night the local lads had moved into the tavern and were now drinking that place dry. They lit a few fires because the company had turned off the power to the place and they had no light.

At just after six the riot police attacked. Unfortunately, one spectator had a bugle and played a few notes. We all shouted 'Charge!' and they did. They were merciless and it was all over in less than 20 minutes as they went through Karoona and the tavern and chased the stragglers up the hill behind.

The cops were dressed in riot gear complete with all the bells, whistles, shields, crash helmets, visors, body armour and boots. The local workers wore shorts and T shirts and were probably barefoot. The squad was stone cold sober and the boys were a 'spark too much'. This meant the beating probably didn't hurt the boys as much as it might otherwise have done, but more than a few would wake up the next day with one hell of a hangover.

Trucks were brought around and the offenders unceremoniously dumped into them to be taken down to Loloho. I don't know what happened down there—I could only imagine—but it was a few days before the lads started coming back to the mine.

The guy with the bugle was sacked on the spot for inciting a volatile situation, and we returned to work. Because there were very few local workers available, we got as much overtime as we wanted, so we made up all the money we lost over the New Year kafuffle.

That riot turned out to be the first of many. Even in the mid-70s the writing was on the wall, yet the Moresby business class continued to abuse the people of Bougainville by flaunting their wealth. It all came to a head in 1989 when the land owners had finally had enough and eventually closed the place down.

40

Pub Island at last

More than once we had tried to get down to the coast, especially over to Pub Island, but we had always been thwarted for one reason or another. Then, just when I was beginning to think we would never make it, Horny bought a boat.

Horny and Harvey were going to be on Bougainville for a while and their passion was fishing, water skiing and just messing about in boats. They had bought a 20 foot cabin cruiser that could sleep four—ideal for running around inside the reef where the water was like a mill pond.

Burgess and I had formed the Skull Island Surf Life Saving Club. It never took off though, mainly because there was no surf and the black sand was full of sand flies. Skull Island was a burial place used by the locals for generations, a tiny island close to the beach where the land dropped off into quite deep water. It came by its name because occasionally a skull or a bone from there found its way on to the beach. Even so, this was an ideal swimming spot.

I think we had two meetings there and both times we

were eaten alive by sand flies. At the first meeting we spotted a shark just off the beach while on the second occasion a body not long committed to the deep washed up quite near to where we were fighting the sand flies. Burgess and I decided to find another location.

Things were changing at work. Whether it was down to us or not is difficult to say, but the plant's output was climbing. We had put a lot of hours into the place and finally had it working as it was designed to work: the plant was humming and the elusive target of 100,000 tons per shift was close to becoming a reality. The only problem was that overtime wasn't as abundant as it had been, and we were not getting the money we had earned when I first arrived.

The company had introduced a 13-day fortnight so we had every second Sunday off. This was good for people like Horny and Harvey who had long-term plans. My plan, however, was to work as much as I could and earn as much as possible in 12 months. These abbreviated weeks hit the pocket, though at the same time I must admit I did enjoy the time off.

It worked both ways. We were supposed to finish at six, but always got away at five on those weekends when we had the Sunday off, which meant we reached the coast before it got dark. We had booked into Millionaire's Row, a row of cabins right on the beach at Loloho. They were let on a first-come-best-dressed basis, and somehow we had managed to snag four of them.

We got down to there just in time to see the sun disappearing behind the mountains, its glow reflected dramatically on the ocean. I never tired of being down at the coast at that time of day, and if the rain stayed away as it had on that particular evening, it was as beautiful a sunset as you would find anywhere in the world.

We had tea at the Loloho mess and made a nuisance of ourselves at the Coastal Club. Before turning in we thought we'd see how difficult it was riding a motor bike with the pillion sitting facing backwards. Somehow this manoeuvre had become known as the 'Lancaster' which required a third person to stand between the 'pilot' and the 'rear gunner.' We had managed this with varying degrees of success, although it always ended with the three of us crashing to the ground and losing some more bark.

On this particular occasion I went head first into the gravel but because we were slightly inebriated I felt nothing. That night I dived into the pillow and was out like a light. I woke up the next morning to find I couldn't see anything.

'I'm blind,' I cried, 'I'm blind.' Putting my hands to my eyes I realised the pillow had stuck to my face.

Burgess who was sharing the room with me couldn't contain himself. 'I wish I had a camera.' I heard him say.

I pulled the pillow off and he laughed even harder. 'You look all patchy like Mikhail Gorbachev.' There were no mirrors in the cabin so I took his word for it.

We loaded up the boat and headed for the horizon about seven thirty on a beautiful morning. Despite a hangover and a few sore limbs I felt in mint condition as I baited a hook and trawled it behind the boat. There were six of us—Captain Horny, First Mate Harvey, Able Seamen Burgess, Rommel and Harpo, and Sub-Lieutenant Seb.

We had all day so we took our time. With Horny at the controls we trawled at an appropriate speed and I caught our first fish, a tuna about 400 millimetres long.

'We'll use that for bait later Harpo,' Horny scoffed.

'No you won't, I'm taking him home.'

Reaching Pub Island we moored just off the beach and came ashore. It was well worth the wait—a magnificent setting. The hotel-resort had been built during the construction of the port and provided an excellent getaway. I fell in love with the place immediately.

'People actually lived here, went to work by boat every morning and came back to this every night?' I asked in disbelief.

'Yep,' Burgess confirmed. He'd been working on Bougainville at the time of the construction. 'Someone had to do it.'

'Must have been awful.'

'Shocking. We came out here at weekends, but there were hundreds out here including too many Septic's (septic tanks = Yanks), so I ended up staying in Panguna.'

We'd brought one esky for the fish we were going to catch and one for the beer. Harvey and Horny wanted to take the boat out over the reef, an offer I declined as I knew there would be plenty of time to mess about in boats later, and I wanted to explore the island. Rommel felt the same way, so after the boys left, the two of us set off to explore Pub Island. It took us about 15 minutes.

The bar didn't open until mid-day (the same licensing hours that applied in Melbourne also applied here) so Rommel and I were at a bit of a loss as to what to do in the meantime. Then we saw the outrigger.

For me, seeing the outrigger canoe pulled up onto the beach was like being presented with a full-size snooker table with all the balls in position and the light switched on, or by a brand new Ferrari in the garage with the keys on a hook on the wall. The outrigger was saying, 'Use me, use me.'

We managed to pull the heavy canoe into the surf, climbed aboard and started rowing. The trouble was that the current in the channel between the island and the mainland ran very swiftly—far too swift to row against—so we had to go with the current. I was surprised at just how fast we were moving and even more surprised when the bark rope that tied the outrigger to the canoe started to unravel. We were unable to prevent the outrigger breaking loose and the second it did so the canoe rolled over, dumping us in the ocean.

I had just finished reading *Jaws*, and the memory of the shark we saw in Buin and the knowledge that I was in shark-infested waters, scared the life out of me. I was never the strongest of swimmers (it had taken me nearly an hour to get my 25 yards' certificate), and I don't think Rommel was much better.

Clinging to the upturned hull in the strongest part of the current we were moving rapidly out to the open sea. I adopted Rommel's credo: 'If in doubt, panic.'

'HELP!' I only screamed for about five minutes when who should come zooming around the corner in his brand new boat but John Bradford, our foreman. I had never been more glad to see him.

He came alongside, threw a rope and towed us back to Pub Island. Rommel somehow managed to get aboard John's boat while I ended up sitting astride the upturned canoe. Every now and then the nose would dip below the surface and I'd go under for a second or two before coming up again to the laughter of everyone in John's boat. Oh yes, very funny!

By the time we arrived back at the island the bar was open, Horny and the boys had returned, and a few others of the boating fraternity had turned up. It seemed that Pub Island was a popular stop off for almost everyone. They cooked a good barbecue and served a very cold beer there, all they had to do was a bit of work on their nautical craft and they had me.

41

Sweet revenge

People come and people go and familiar faces were soon forgotten as others took their places. Uncle Ron was leaving. He had rekindled my passion for motorbikes and was without doubt the best motorcyclist I had ever ridden with. I not only learned a lot of the basic tricks from him but he also taught me to get up and get back on again when I came off.

We had a going away party for Ron and all of us went down to the airport to see him off. Then we had a feed at Black Joe's, the tiny eatery that was fast gaining a reputation as the best restaurant on the island. The Davara Motel had recently opened so we spent the night there. The first floor balcony of the Davara made an excellent diving platform into the pool below. The second floor would have been even better except the motel didn't have one.

Ron departed and a curious little Scotsman replaced him. We watched Ron's plane take off and disappear. It was just after nine but we were in no hurry to return to work. We had developed an attitude with the powers-that-be that if they wanted to mess with our hours we'd mess with them too. They still asked us to work longer when it suited them and being ready to sell our souls for money we always obliged, but we also enjoyed our little bit of defiance.

We saddled up and were about to head off up the hill when I first noticed him. The human resources staff were currently losing about two men a week, so they usually made every effort to meet new arrivals and get them off on the right foot. This bloke must have slipped through the net somehow.

'Where are you headed, mate?' I asked.

'Bougainville,' he told me, his Scottish accent so thick you could cut it.

'Can you be a bit more specific?'

'BCL.'

'Well, that's close enough: we're the welcoming committee.'

He stood about five feet, a strange looking individual with tight curly hair. His bulging Marty Feldman eyes made him look like a gecko and before he had put his kit in the back of Burgess's Jeep, he had been named accordingly. I think it was a record.

He offered his hand to Rommel. 'Eric ...' he started to introduce himself.

'No mate, you are now Gecko,' Rommel told him and we took him to the Pink Palace.

We dispatched him at Davo's office but he reappeared before the end of the day as I knew he would. I was called to John Bradford's office where we met again and we became the best of mates for the next four months.

Gecko was a good tradesman who could turn his hand to almost anything, much like the rest of us. Even though we were all in our mid-20s and well out of our apprenticeships, we were realising there was a long way to go before we became fully 'multi-skilled'. Gecko hit the ground running and slipped right into our little group.

We were on the cusp of some big changes. Maintenance

planners and schedulers were arriving and 'maintenance by crisis' was becoming a thing of the past. Instead of putting out fires, we now had a daily plan and our days were becoming more and more structured. We worked 10 hour days, six days a week with every Sunday off. If you wanted to work a Sunday you had to put your name down, and if there was something that urgently needed doing you would get a few extra hours.

This was the beginning of the end as far as I was concerned. As happy as I was for them that their plant was finally working, I wasn't there for the kudos, I was there for the money.

Wayne the Crane put in his notice after two years and I landed his job looking after all the overhead cranes on the plant. It was a magic little number and I soon learned that no one knew or cared what I did during the day as long as they had uninterrupted 24/7 crane coverage.

With just a tiny adjustment I learned how to ensure that the brakes on the cranes needed regular attention and I was back to working 12 hours a day with the occasional double shift thrown in for a rope change. If I needed an offsider, Gecko was my man. We both worked a 70 hour week and I was happy again.

The planners had a lot of work in front of them but to their credit and with our reluctant help we slowly got the place working properly, finally hitting the elusive target of a 100,000 ton shift. Amman Charlie, the man in charge of the shift that set the record, could never have hit the target without us. He became such a pain in the ass bragging about his achievement that I locked him in a shipping container for 10 hours.

Amman Charlie, as his name suggests, was an Arab from Jordan and like most operations foremen he took some kind of sadistic delight in driving the plant into the ground and then complaining he couldn't work because his tools were broken. When Amman accepted his award for setting the record he said in his speech that on many occasions that he had been close to the target but the maintenance department had let him down.

'You'll get yours,' I said to myself and I was surprised how quickly I found my chance to repay him. Just the next day, as I was servicing a hoist in the screen house, I spotted him going out to one of the supply containers. I couldn't believe my luck. He was inside doing a stock take when all of a sudden the door shut!

I got a call telling me that a particular crane was available for a long overdue service, so off I went and for the rest of the day I completely forgot about Amman. Inside the shipping container it would have been like an oven. I thought someone would have found him but at about four o'clock I drove past the container and it was still as I had left it, with the lock and keys on one of the handles. Gecko nipped over to it, unlocked the doors and scarpered. Up in the screen house I watched Amman stumble out in quite a state. It couldn't have happened to a nicer bloke.

42

Over the hill

Things were changing on every front. After Burgess returned from annual leave he was transferred to help set up the company's new training department. It became one of the best trade schools in the southern hemisphere and any tradesman who had served his time with Bougainville Copper was very sought after.

Rommel transferred to the truck shop, working with Big Danny. Bagdad was still with us but seemed to be just going through the motions. Harvey and Horny were content with their boat and a five-day week. More new faces arrived including Rambo and Harrington who became good friends, but the original gang had gone and so had much of the passion.

Long before construction started on the Panguna Processing Plant there had been a small mine up on the ridge that overlooked the town, a kind of a pilot plant built after the war. Of the few people who had climbed up there in search of El Dorado most had either come back saying they couldn't find it or hadn't come back at all and had to be rescued. Although no-one was ever seriously hurt, a night in the jungle had a profound effect on those who experienced it, and caused a few red faces.

Gecko wanted to go up there so we made plans. As soon as word got around Rambo and a few more of the blokes were keen to come too, and before we knew it half a dozen of us were setting off on our little adventure.

It had been a bad week for overtime. My logic was that the week was lost anyway and I'd start again next week, so I took the Saturday and the Sunday off. Early on the Saturday morning, we all met up at Kawarong, ate a hearty breakfast and headed up to the end of town.

Before we had even left the road it was obvious this was going to be quite a hike. I looked at the motley crew I was with. All were smoking and even though it wasn't yet eight o'clock, two or three had cracked open the first can of the day. Oh yeah, this had all the ingredients, I thought to myself.

The rough track that led from the back of Married Hill up into the bush covering the foothills very soon became difficult to follow. Climbing up the face of the ridge that overlooked the town, we had plenty of time to enjoy the magnificent view, because we stopped for a smoke break every 20 minutes, then every 10. We could only move as fast as our slowest man, and as a consequence it took us over three hours to reach the peak of the range. Still, I thought this was quite an achievement considering we had smoked a packet of cigarettes and drunk the best part of a carton of SP Greenies getting there.

From our rough map of how to reach the mine I estimated that we were just about half way. Already a little voice in my head was telling me we were not going to find the place, and should get back before nightfall, but we pushed common sense aside and continued down the other side of the range. We reached the valley just as the clouds rolled in. It grew darker and the rain started. Having strayed from the track, we very quickly found ourselves slipping and stumbling through the thick wet jungle, hopelessly lost.

The clouds rolled through the forest like a fog but we were all still together. That was the only positive thing I could think of. We had lost all sight of the sun and the rain beat down as hard as ever, as we continued down to the foot of the valley. Then, incredibly, we stumbled upon the old mine. It simply appeared out of the mist and rain before us. To have succeeded where most of the intrepid adventurers from Panguna had failed was no small consolation. The remains of an old cone crusher we found made Gecko quite excited when he discovered where it came from.

'Look at this Harpo, made in Scotland,' he said proudly.

Rambo was very happy for him as he sat in the rain looking at what we had spent six hours coming to see.

'We've come all this way to see a Scottish crusher,' Rambo said finally.

'Have you seen one before?' Gecko asked. 'They don't make them anymore.'

'I wonder why.'

The little voice in my head had been right. It was now dark, very wet and getting late. After the minor high of finding the mine, the reality of the situation returned.

'I think we should stay here for the night,' I suggested. 'We'll never find our way out in the dark. We have a vague idea of where we are and in the morning we can just retrace our tracks back up to the ridge.'

Mal, who had been scouting around while he still could, returned to the group.

'Come with me, I've found something.'

He had discovered a shed that might once have been a small workshop. There was nothing inside except a pile of rubbish and some tyres in one corner but the main thing was the shed was dry.

'Just one minor detail.' Mal told us.

'What's that?' I asked.

'The python in the corner.'

It was the biggest snake I'd ever seen. Initially I thought

it was a pile of old tyres. I don't have a problem with snakes, and pythons aren't poisonous, but there was just something about sleeping in a room with a monster like this only a couple of metres away that didn't appeal.

'We could always move it,' suggested Mal.

'How?' Gecko wanted to know.

'Smoke him out.'

And that is what we did. We had brought a lot of rubbish with us, and once we got a fire going there was plenty of green stuff around to generate a bit of smoke. It worked a treat because as soon as he got whiff of the smoke old Monty decided his new roommates could have the place to themselves and slithered across the floor towards the open door. He was the length of the shed (which Rambo paced as six metres), and as round as a small dinner plate, yet placid as anything. I almost felt sorry for him as we closed the door behind him.

I've had worse nights' sleep but I've had a lot better too. After there was no more material to keep the fire going we sat in the darkness and talked until we ran out of beer, and cigarettes as well. Trying to ignore the noises outside (I thought the python might have returned and brought a few of his mates), we gradually dropped off and the long night slowly came to an end.

About seven, after a very ordinary breakfast, the sun finally started to penetrate the dense bush and we felt it was time to head off. Our intention was to return to Panguna by retracing our steps to the top of the range, once up there we figured we'd find a track and follow it back down the other side. But only a few minutes after we set off we came across a very well-worn path leading in the opposite direction so it made sense to follow it. An hour or so later we came to a gorge with a river running through it and a small village on the opposite bank. We were no longer lost.

The village elders were becoming used to small parties stumbling across their settlement, and after we explained who we were they made us welcome, offering us a bite to eat.

Next we followed the path that took us right into Sid Wyatt's back garden. Sid was one of the new breed of planners who had recently arrived and he was having a bit of trouble fitting in. He couldn't believe his luck when six of the guys he would love to have fitted in with arrived at his back door.

'You haven't got a beer on you have you Sid?' Rambo asked. Of course he had.

We drank a couple with Sid, then went on to see Harrington who lived just down the road. We set about cleaning out his fridge.

'They've got the army out looking for you lot,' Harrington told us.

'Better get some more beer then, John.' Rambo suggested.

'Why's that then?' he asked.

'It could be days before they find us here.'

43

My dad in the Blitz

—ഇരുജ—

My dad was 17 years and 63 days old when the Second World War broke out. Because he was too young to go to war, the war came to him courtesy of the Luftwaffe. It didn't arrive straight away, mind, he had to wait 53 weeks, but on September 7 1940 the war quite literally came to my dad's front room.

He was an apprentice sheet metal worker at the time, working in the London docks installing ventilation ducts in ships converted into troop carriers. On the fateful day he went to a dance in the city's West End with his best mate Fred Clements (my future godfather). During the evening the air raid sirens sounded. After hitting Hull and the ports on the east coast in daring daylight raids, German bombers were apparently targeting London in their first night-time attack.

The dance finished early and I guess dad hadn't scored, because he and Freddy walked through the back streets on their way to Westminster Bridge. From there they looked down the river towards the East End. 'It seemed like all of East London was on fire,' he told me years later.

With the roads either closed or simply impassable, it took him two hours to walk from Westminster to his home in Rotherhithe, but when he turned into his street he found it barricaded and guarded.

'I want to go home, I live here,' he told the policeman guarding the barricade.

'Where do you live?' The copper asked him.

'Reid Street.'

'Reid Street's gone, son.'

My dad was completely shocked. 'What d'you mean gone?'

'There's nothing left, it's been blown to pieces. Any survivors were taken to Russell Street School.' His old school— Dad knew where that was. Ten minutes later he found himself at another barricade guarded by another policeman.

'I need to get to Russell Street School,' he told the policeman.

'It's gone son, took a direct hit.'

'What about the people who were sheltering there?' he asked, not really wanting to hear the answer.'

'I don't know ... I'm sorry ....'

Dad was lost, stunned. When he had left that morning to catch the bus with his older brother Harry, his mum and dad were having breakfast at the kitchen table and his sister was in the scullery doing the laundry. Now they were all gone. Had they really all gone? He was having trouble getting his head around the facts that confronted him.

All night long, as they pulled bodies from the rubble, he helped where he could.

'Not really dressed for it are you lad?' someone commented looking at the suit and polished shoes he was wearing for dancing.

'How do you dress for this sort of thing?' he asked, completely numb. He couldn't believe he'd lost everyone.

When the sun came up, the full extent of what had happened started to become apparent. There was total devastation, entire neighbourhoods gone, fires burning out of control. Everywhere he looked he saw that the war had finally arrived.

To try to take his mind off of his own horrible situation he continued helping until mid-morning, when he went looking in the only place left he could think of—his older sister Ginny's place. With the whole area still burning, he finally gave up trying to get through on foot and took a river taxi down the Thames to Tower Bridge near Ginny's tiny flat. That part of the city had been bombed too, but among the chaos he eventually found the flat—with all his family in it.

'Where have you been?' his mother asked. 'I've been worried sick.'

—ᔆᘛᘺᔆ—

44

Stunned angel fish

Rommel, Rambo, Harrington and I sat outside the Costal Club admiring the blush in the eastern sky. The sun was rising over the Pacific and the beautiful morning wasn't lost on us despite the considerable amount we had drunk during the night. None of us had scored (just as well as both Rambo and Harrington were married) but we'd enjoyed ourselves.

'Every day is like a new birth,' mused Rommel. He was no more drunk than the rest of us, just more philosophical.

'Y'know, I think this might be an excellent day to go fishing,' suggested Harrington.

He had brought up the idea many times over the months we had worked together, but this really was an ideal opportunity. We drained our last stubbies, jumped into Rommel's Landcruiser and drove over to Harrington's place.

Harrington was one of those people who preferred his surname to his first and if my name had been Julian I would have chosen Harrington as well. He was the foreman in the pit workshop in charge of the maintenance of most of the mobile equipment at the mine, and because of his position he had quite a nice house with an ocean view not far from the club.

In a few minutes we were hitching up Harrington's 16-foot aluminium boat and loading it with the requirements of a busy day on the water, including ice and beer, rods and reels—and a few guns. We then drove on to Rambo's place.

Rambo was another one of those blokes who had fitted right in as soon as he arrived on site. We called him Rambo because he told us to and until this day I've never found out his real name. He worked as a fitter underground and had access to the blasting equipment. Over a few weeks he had managed to bring to the surface half a dozen sticks of dynamite, detonators, and a reel or two of blasting wire. We must have made some noise loading these into the back of the car because we managed to wake Raelene, Rambo's wife.

'What's going on Rambo?'

She stood at the top of the stairs in her dressing gown, arms folded, looking very formidable.

'We're going fishing dear,' Rambo told her honestly.

'With a shotgun, a rifle and box of dynamite?' She was coming down a few stairs for a good look in the back of the car.

'And a couple of rods, sweet thing.'

'If you're not home by lunchtime I'm calling the police,' Raelene threatened as she stomped back upstairs.

'I got out of that a lot cheaper than I thought,' he said to himself as much as anyone else.

When we reached the boat ramp it wasn't as busy as I'd expected at that time of the morning so we were able to load everything into the boat without any curious eyes watching us. The outboard motor kicked into life and we set off across the harbour and out to the reef. With hardly a ripple rocking the boat we reached the horizon in no time.

Harrington who was driving the boat slowed as the water began to chop a bit over the reef. Then, when we were almost out of sight of land, we turned off the engine and started fishing.

We set about preparing the first charge, but a beer was in order first. We all popped a can as Rambo pulled a stick of dynamite from its packet. Harrington cut the stick in half with his filleting knife and pushed a detonator into the putty while Rommel and I ran out about 30 metres of detonating cord. Harrington connected the bare ends to the detonator, wrapped the little package up in a plastic bag, and threw it out of the back of the boat.

With the throttle open we trawled the bomb behind us, then we slowed down and the little bundle slipped beneath the surface. When Rommel bared the other end of the detonating cord and placed both wires on the battery terminal there was just a strange, dull thud. We turned the boat around, trawled over to where the blast had occurred and ran around the area for a few minutes, but nothing came to the surface except a couple of stunned angel fish.

'Nah!' snorted Rommel, 'we need more dynamite.' Everyone agreed, although none of us had ever done this before. A full stick was needed, we decided, and we went through the procedure of putting a bomb together once again while knocking back another can.

Now a more significant thump shook the boat and produced a small splash behind us. We turned the boat around, convinced we would find something worth taking home but again the rewards were trifling.

Opting to try a different part of the reef we settled back with another can while Harrington opened up the throttle and bounced us across the sea once more. About 10 minutes later he slowed at what seemed as good a place as any.

The decision was to use two sticks of dynamite and to try and to sink the bomb as close to the reef as possible. This time when Rommel detonated it there was a massive thump, and the spray from the blast blew water, bits of sea life and a lot of coral over the boat and its occupants.

'That's more like it!' said Rommel throwing a chunk of coral out of the boat.

Soon a couple of yellow fin tuna floated to the top plus a few unfamiliar species. If nothing else we would have a good feed of fresh tuna. After a few more minutes that did indeed appear to be the sum total sum produced by the blast so we had another can.

'So what d'you reckon, shall we use the rest of the dynamite on the last explosion or on two smaller ones?' asked Harrington. We decided to use the lot, except we didn't seem to have much detonating cord left.

'We've got enough,' said Rommel confidently, but I wasn't so sure.

We ran off what I estimated to be about 10 foot!

'Plenty,' Rommel confirmed. Harrington put the last charge together and threw the bag out the back of the boat. For some reason he also backed off the throttle which caused the engine to cough and stop and left us drifting back a little. Largely unaware of the lack of forward movement Rommel proceeded to bare the wires, detonate the charge, and blew us right out of the fucking water!

There was an almighty blast right underneath us. It was like the world was in slow motion as we made cartwheels upwards—Harrington, me, a few angel fish and a lot of coral.

Miraculously the boat came down the right way up and I plunged into the water about 10 feet away. I surfaced, followed by Rambo, and we both swam to the boat. I managed to haul myself up and then pulled in Rambo. Rommel, on the other side a few feet away, came swimming towards us too. The three of us were OK apart from being a bit beaten around the edges but the same couldn't be said for our skipper. Harrison seemed to have come down face first inside the boat. He was out for the count.

'We'd better head in,' Rambo suggested.

We took stock of what we had lost. The esky, what remained of the beer, and our catch, were all gone: just the guns remained where we had stowed them. Going to the back of the boat to start the engine I discovered we were out of fuel and that the jerry can had gone overboard too. But most important, which way was home?

We figured that we had come out almost due east so we thought that if we headed west we'd get back. Right now though it was late morning and the sun was almost directly overhead so we wouldn't know where west was until a bit later in the day.

Our previously light-hearted mood became quite sombre as the gravity of the situation descended upon us. The sun was becoming fiercer, and with no cover on the boat we were all showing the first signs of sunburn. A bigger concern still was the complete lack of water. After drinking alcohol for over 18 hours, we were starting to feel thirsty and the real fear of dehydration was not far away. We were drifting when a noise caused me to look over the side. Right beside us, bumping against the hull, was a very stunned but quite impressive eight foot hammer-head shark!

'We have company lads,' I said, but no one was interested.

I tied the shark to the side of the boat and waited. By the afternoon the sun was at its hottest. There wasn't even the hint of a breeze and with nowhere to hide, we were really suffering from the heat and thirst. Harrington remained unconscious. Slowly two o'clock became three and three became four. It was now very obvious which way west was, but the last two hours had taken its toll on us.

'This is stupid,' I thought to myself. We couldn't be more than 10 miles from land and we needed to start making some kind of effort to get home.

I guess Rommel felt the same. 'Fancy rowing?' he asked.

For a few minutes the two of us made a futile attempt to row a 16 foot boat with our hands! The exertion made us feel even worse. The shark, still tied to the side of the boat, didn't exactly make things any easier either.

The sun was disappearing in the far western sky but it had done a lot of damage. I lay in the bottom of the boat until, lulled by its gentle rocking, I dropped off to sleep. I wasn't well and my sleep was very disturbed, fraught with nightmares, rocking and crashing ....

What the f... ! I was woken by the wash of the *Bougainville Maru* that almost swamped us. After half an hour's sleep I felt refreshed and relieved as the big ore carrier slowed to pick us up. A small launch was lowered and in the fading light some of the crew came across to help us, bringing us water. After we'd recovered enough to transfer Harrington into the launch and tie ourselves to their stern, they towed us to the ship.

Half an hour later Harrington was being treated in their sick bay while Rambo and I were on deck watching Rommel tie the derrick hoist rope around the tail of the big fish. Just as they started hoisting the bloody thing woke up, and it wasn't even slightly impressed. The Japanese crewmen thought it was hilarious as they hoisted the fighting hammerhead over the rail.

But Rommel soon put a stop to the struggle. He strode across the deck with the automatic pistol in his hand and shot the shark through the head. It was then lowered onto the deck and a few photos were taken of us with our trophy.

Our boat was finally winched up, and as the pilot came aboard to take the ship into the wharf, the Japanese captain joined us on deck. We stood at the starboard rail as the pilot guided the ship into its mooring and I waved to Rambo's wife and Maureen Harrington in the small crowd that had gathered to welcome us home.

The captain looked inside our boat and pulled out the fishing rod, the only one in there. 'Who caught the fish?' he asked in perfect English. It wasn't a casual question and he looked for an answer.

'Harrington,' the three of us replied in unison, indicating the man in their sick bay.

'Unbelievable,' the captain muttered. 'Unbelievable', he repeated, 'this fish must weigh over two hundred kilos and he caught it on a 10 pound line and with a hook the size of a nickel? I have heard many fishing stories but I believe this is the most ... (he searched for the word he wanted but failed) ... unbelievable.'

'Absolutely,' I agreed.

45

Pulley problem

After a high seas rescue one week and getting lost in the jungle the next, it was almost a welcome relief to return to the mundane duties of crusher maintenance. A couple of double shifts over the next two weeks produced enough overtime to bolster the bank account. Then there was a shutdown.

The head drum on the No. 2 conveyor needed replacing, a big 16-hour job and one that hadn't been done before. Because I was the senior fitter who'd done a few smaller pulley replacements, they decided I was their man. The trouble was, this was a massive pulley with massive bearings in a 400 mm shaft, and I knew that we didn't have the right tools for the job.

A couple of days before the shutdown, preparing for the job with one of the apprentices, I put the bearings on the new pulley and measured everything up. But when it came to tightening up the bearings we struggled all day. In the end I had to tell my bosses that without the proper tools we couldn't get anywhere near the recommended clearance level.

They didn't want to know. The message came back that we were to tighten the bearings as much as possible. We needed a hydraulic nut and we were using flogging spanners.

On the big day it was like a three ringed circus. Planners, schedulers and trainers were watching us, taking photos, writing up a list of all the tools we used and recording the procedure. My old mate Harvey was working with me and we were very pleased to get the old pulley out and the new one installed within 12 hours—just in time to make it to the tavern for last orders.

But at two o'clock the next morning I heard an ominous knock on my door.

'Harpo, your pulley has moved!' It was Horny taking great delight in waking me with this little bit of news I didn't want to hear.

I went up to the top of the springboard with him and sure enough the pulley had moved. In fact it had moved so far it was rubbing against the superstructure.

'Oh fuck!'

The result was another six hours of hard graft followed by the Nuremburg Trial Mark II, a disciplinary hearing where my bosses, who all happened to be German, ducked any responsibility and gave me a Disciplinary Action (DA) for negligence. 'We ver celebrating an early finish to der shutdown because the pulley vos fitted quickly yar, but I don't see much reason for celebrating now,' complained KKK, our new foreman.

I resented it. They were saying I was not a good tradesman and I knew I was better than any of those at the hearing. Bitterly disappointed I went back to the cranes and kept out of everyone's way. I had toyed with the idea of taking a short break at the end of my first contract, then coming back to do another 12 months. Not anymore. I had outstayed my welcome and was really ready to go.

Rommel left a week before me. He and Ron were going to fly to Singapore, buy a couple of bikes, head up the Malay peninsula and try to ride back to England. Rommel almost succeeded in convincing me to join them, but I decided I still had a lot to do in this part of the world, so I declined his offer.

We gave Rommel the same send off as Uncle Ron, with tea at Black Joe's followed by a party at the Davara, using the pool as the centrepiece. We had a final beer with Rommel at the airport and that was it. I was going to miss him more than anyone. He was reliable, honest, a bloody good tradesman and possibly the funniest man I've ever worked with. Thirty years later we are still the best of mates.

Although I had arrived in Bougainville with lots of enthusiasm and a can-do attitude, I was leaving feeling tired and cynical. I knew I was a better tradesman for having been there and I'd made some great friends, but I think the endless hours of working had finally taken their toll. Now it was time to find another adventure.

I had been talking to a couple of blokes who told me to try construction and one night in my room, starting to plan my next trip, I pencilled a few places to phone. Then, listening to Bob Seger singing *Main Street*, I dropped off to sleep.

I dreamt I was on a train being rocked to sleep with the motion of the carriage, but the rocking became quite violent and I woke up to find the whole place gyrating. The glass window slats were twisting, breaking and falling out of their slots onto the floor. The stereo speakers fell off of the shelf above me onto my bed and I heard smashing glass and noise all around me. Holy shit, this was an earthquake—a *guria* as they called them in New Guinea. I jumped up, pulled on a pair of shorts, and quickly joined the frightened crowd in the corridor evacuating the building.

'If in doubt, panic!' Rommel's famous quote rang in my ears.

'YUHULYU!' shouted the local boys as they often did when they got a little excited. We ran along the corridor, down the stairs and across the road to a piece of open ground outside the supermarket. Feeling safe there, we were chatting excitedly when I happened to notice Happy Frank, all 24 stone of him. Happy wore a crash helmet and the biggest pair of underpants I'd ever seen. As the ground continued to shake with the aftershocks he quivered like a huge jelly—a priceless sight.

With the aftershocks continuing all night, a few of us braved the tremors and brought the contents of our fridges across the road to hold a guria party.

I sold my motor bike the next day for $500 dollars—not a bad price given that I'd paid $1200 for it and had put it through the wringer. I had nicknamed the bike Hero after the ghost's horse in the *Phantom* comics.

'You look after Hero.' I told the buyer. 'God knows, I didn't.'

46

Next stop Fiji

On my last day I was sent down to Loloho to help out on a shutdown there and Burgess gave me a ride down to the coast in his jeep. I checked out of Karawong, saying goodbye to Jimmy Tulumby who had been a good mate for the better part of a year. I gave him all of the kina change I'd saved, my records and record player.

The shutdown proved to be a non-event. We were finished by about four thirty, at which point I removed my locks and tags, packed up my toolbox and said my farewells.

My going-away party was possibly the smallest I'd ever attended. There weren't many of the old crowd left, although all the people who mattered turned up including Burgess, Gecko, Harvey, Horny, Rambo, Harrington, plus a couple of new starters. For the first time in three visits to the Davara, I actually slept in a room that I'd paid for.

The plane to Honiara left at nine and we arrived with plenty of time. The Moresby flight had just deposited another couple of new starters who looked around apprehensively, not sure if they'd done the right thing.

'You'll be alright lads; you won't know yourselves after a year,' I tried helpfully, but I don't think my ploy worked because they ran off urgently seeking someone who could offer them a return ticket. My flight was called, there were stiff handshakes all around, I gave Gecko a kiss and quickly left. Even though I really wanted to go, the departure, as always, was difficult for me.

I arrived in Honiara at lunch time, booking into the Mendana Hotel right down on the beach. I then spent a lazy day between the beach and the bar with the firm intention of spending all my four days there in exactly the same way.

I had been fascinated with Guadalcanal since I first heard the name and now I stood on the beach made famous by John Wayne in his war film. Thirty years after World War II, there were still many scars and reminders of what had happened here. The airport was called Henderson Field after Major Lofton Henderson, a marine killed during the Battle of Midway. It was the airfield the Allies wanted, a stepping stone towards Japan.

In the hills behind the town were caves where the Japanese dug in. It was rumoured there were still a few old soldiers around who hadn't surrendered, but I didn't see them as I climbed up there.

After I got back to the Mendana I ran into a drunken school teacher in the bar who offered to lend me his motor cycle. It was too good an offer to knock back so I rode the bike as far to the east as I could until the road turned to dirt. I would have gone into the bush except that doing it without Rommel and the boys seemed dull. When I got back to the Mendana it was dark and the school teacher had gone, but the bar staff knew him quite well and someone took his bike home. He was a sad man—a reminder that not everyone enjoys these romantic and mysterious places.

I went snorkelling the next day with a small party, diving over a few wrecks. I managed to get over my fear of claustrophobia when snorkelling and my morbid fear of sharks too, because we saw literally schools of them. Wearing a life jacket I lay on top of the water on my stomach and floated around looking at the splendour just below the surface.

It was such an interesting day that when I returned to the hotel in the evening I fell asleep exhausted. I never knew floating could be so tiring.

My next stop was Fiji. I left Honiara in the afternoon and it was late in the evening when we approached Nadi. As we were flying through a rain storm, lightning lit up the sky and it seemed we were being bounced all over the place. I don't know what I'd expected to see when I'd booked my window seat, but I was rewarded with a stunning light show.

As we descended through the clouds the rain seemed to fall harder than ever and the turbulence got worse until, all of a sudden, there was the runway before us. No sooner had we hit the ground when, to my alarm, we started to accelerate and took off again. The cabin crew looked quite alarmed too as we again circled the airport, dropped, hit still more turbulence, shook and then descended again. Fortunately this time we stayed on the ground and taxied to the terminal. Apparently on our first landing attempt a herd of cows had wandered onto the runway.

In the pouring rain outside the arrivals hall, while most of the passengers seemed to join friends waiting for them, I hailed one of the few old taxis looking for business.

'Where to sir?' The taxi driver asked.

I had nothing booked and the only hotel in Suva I knew of was the Grand Old Lady.

'The Grand Pacific please.'

The Grand Pacific Hotel had been built before World War I by a big shipping company. Any passenger staying there would have felt they'd never gone ashore because the rooms resembled the staterooms of grand ocean liners. It was a magnificent old colonial hotel and a bargain at $10 a night.

My bedroom was massive—I'm sure I could have played five-a-side in there. Queen Victoria, I was told, had stayed in this very room, which I doubted as she had died 15 years before the hotel was built. Still, the room was certainly made for royalty. It had a big old bath tub that took about a fortnight to fill. I put just enough in to wash myself, then lay on top of the massive four-poster bed in the darkness, listening to the rain.

The next morning I had breakfast outside my room, on an enormous veranda that ran right around the hotel like the deck of a ship. Yesterday's storm had blown out to sea and I had a glorious view across to the harbour and out to the island on the horizon. Finally, I thought, I might have found paradise. I had all sorts of plans, but my first was to secure this room for however long I decided to stay.

47

Dinner on a yacht

Having extended my stay by a couple of nights I went in search of any island tours that could expand on my Solomon's experience as a master snorkler. There were day trips available to Treasure Island and Castaway Island, so I booked myself on both of those, ready to make the most of the really good weather forecast for the next week.

The harbour was a fascinating place with a market doing a brisk trade in ersatz island stuff, and craft including a yacht out of Mooloolaba, another out of Santa Catalina, a third from Auckland and a cruise ship. The pub is always the spot to meet interesting people, I've found, and this place was no exception. People-watching at the bar, I was well into my second beer when the barman asked, 'You looking for a job?'

'Not really, I've just finished a job up in New Guinea.'

'What d'you do?'

'Fitter and turner.'

'Not much call for fitters and turners,' he told me.

'That's good to hear.'

But he was wrong. By the end of the morning I could

have had any number of jobs except that money was rubbish. Apparently people were quite happy to work for small change just in order to be here, but not me. I was heading for the door when a bloke approached me.

'Are you a machinist?'

'I might be. Why?'

'I have an urgent job. My maintenance man has jumped ship and the barman said you were a turner.'

'What's the problem?'

'Our main water pump, well our only water pump, looks like it's a snapped shaft.'

'Really? Water pumps don't usually shear shaft if they are only pumping water. Can I have a look?'

'Oh I wish you would.'

Five minutes later I found myself in a small speedboat skimming across the harbour water towards an attractive motor yacht moored just off shore. I was received like royalty. A broken-down water pump on this little floating mansion meant they had no drinking water, no water for showering, and none for cooking.

Down in the engine room sat a Worthington centrifugal pump.

'Hey it's a Worthington, they're English, best water pump in the world,' I explained.

'Not at the moment it's not.' Peter countered

The motor spun, but the pump didn't, so I stopped it, removed the guard, started it again and found the problem.

'OK. I can fix this—the key has sheared.'

It looked like a couple of hours' work if they had the right parts, which was unlikely. I would need my toolbox so Peter, the guy who had brought me, sent someone to my hotel to fetch it, while I started taking the pump apart. Once I had the toolbox I was able to make a new puller as well as cutting and fitting a new key, but fresh problems kept coming to light. I ended up having to rebuild a whole number of broken or missing parts and spent the afternoon flushing out debris that had collected in the pump.

The moment of truth came when I turned the motor on: she spun at 1400 rpm and whistled. In just a few moments they had water coming out of their ears. It was one of the most satisfying moments of my life. I know, I need to get out more, but it was a lovely feeling.

Peter who had never been too far away was there to help me clean up.

'Will you stay for dinner?' he asked.

'I'd love to.'

Dinner was a seafood delight with lobster and oysters and some beautiful fish I'd never heard of. It was served in the state room where I felt I was being treated as the guest of honour. This seemed to be a distinctly gay ship which was fine except of course there was not a woman in sight. I was offered the vacant position of ship's engineer but I declined, probably because of the lack of females.

Just before I left the yacht, Peter gave me US$100, the most I had ever been paid for a day's work. Back at the hotel I put the toolbox in the luggage room behind the desk while I went up to the bar. I felt I'd earned a drink and wanted some company.

The moon hung over the harbour on that beautiful evening and a light breeze blew through the open saloon. It was late, almost midnight, and as I ordered a beer I noticed a couple of women sitting at a table.

'Can I buy you ladies a drink?' I asked full of goodwill. They accepted and I joined them. They were a mother and daughter from Sydney, looking for love in all the wrong places I thought.

'Have you had a good day?' I asked.

They said they had, but I doubted it.

'And how was your day?' the daughter asked.

'Magic. See that yacht out there in the harbour?' I began, pointing to the vessel where I'd spent most of the day. 'I had dinner on that tonight.'

The two women, no doubt noticing the dirt under my fingernails, my stained shirt and dirty jeans, looked at me sympathetically, I could tell they didn't believe me and was about to enlarge, but I checked myself. 'Nah', I thought, 'what's the point.' And I've never told anyone that story until now.

48

Five dollars well spent

The next morning I was up early and in the lobby waiting to be taken to the boat bound for Treasure Island. As I sat up front in the sun, read my book and did my best to enjoy the half hour trip, I looked around and counted 15 people—seven couples and me. It dawned on me that this was the sort of thing that couples did, not single hairy-arsed fitters. Anyway I was there now. On this perfect day the breeze took the bite out of the sun and I spent most of the day snorkelling and floating over a coral landscape.

I was possibly as far from London as I could ever get without leaving the planet, and I wondered about Len, Rob, Elaine and my dad. I missed them, but I wouldn't swap this for whatever they were doing. Funny what you think about when you're snorkelling.

I went in for lunch then decided to explore the island. Right around the other side, far from prying eyes, I came across two women, young and attractive but grossly overweight, dressed in shorts and bras.

'How're you going ladies?' I asked.

They went into a flap, embarrassed that I should have seen them.

'What do you want?' They were on the defensive straight away.

'How about a bit of light conversation? It would seem we are the only ones that are not part a couple.'

'How do you know that we aren't a couple?'

'Lesbians? Well don't lesbians need someone to talk to as well?'

'We're not lesbians, we're just ... shy.'

Jean, Nancy and I enjoyed a lovely afternoon snorkelling. I made them laugh, which I don't think happened very often. Before we knew it, our day on Treasure Island had come to an end and we were being herded back to the launch.

As we approached Nandi harbour, Jean and Nancy enquired what I was doing that evening.

'I have no idea.' I replied, thinking of possibly hitting a night club or two.

The girls had discovered that every Tuesday night a bunch of locals and expats got together for an hour of touch football. They asked if I wanted to play.

'Sure, I'll play,' I said, genuinely interested in a run out. Jean and Nancy, I discovered, played rugby for Dunedin Ladies.

'Hookers?' I asked.

They smirked. They gave me directions and I met them later at Albert Park, just across from my hotel. When I got there I was surprised to find almost as many women as men. They split up into teams and I found myself playing against my two new friends.

More people get hurt in touch football than any other game I know, mainly because most of them are unfit, yet still believe they can travel a hundred yards in ten seconds. The other reason is because of the physical nature of the game. The players have to release the ball as soon as they are touched. I was 'touched' twice by Nancy—touches I'll remember for as long as I live!

I don't know who won, but I left the field with a few sore muscles and a great deal of admiration for rugby players, especially female rugby players. After the game we limped back to my hotel and had a drink in the bar. I then gave the concierge five dollars to look the other way while I took Nancy and Jean back to my room. What an excellent five dollar investment that turned out to be.

I was supposed to go to Castaway Island the next day, but the girls wouldn't let me leave. Instead we spent what can only be described as an interesting morning. They left at about midday and I missed them immediately.

The remainder of my stay was unremarkable. I was downstairs the following morning with intentions of taking the trip to Castaway, until I saw all of the honeymoon couples planning to go. I gave it a body swerve, heading for the harbour instead. And that was Fiji. The holiday was over. It was time to go back to work.

ও

My plane left on the Friday afternoon and when I arrived at the airport check in with my 36 kilo toolbox the counter clerk was about to say something, then hesitated.

'Mr Garner, you've been upgraded to Business Class and your luggage has been cleared.' I was as surprised as the woman.

She gave me my boarding pass and a voucher to get me into the Business Class lounge. This was how I liked to travel. I liked it even more when I was greeted like a VIP in the lounge.

I was handed an envelope from Peter, the man I did the work for aboard the yacht, with a note that explained everything. The vessel belonged to a Fijian dignitary and this was his way of thanking me for the work I had done.

Pouring myself a large whiskey I raised my glass in a quiet toast.

'You're welcome.'

49

Return to Melbourne

I flew into Melbourne on August 6 1975. Not having shaved or had a haircut in the 54 weeks I'd been away I bore no resemblance to the picture in my passport and, being a Pom, I wasn't surprised that the customs and immigration people enjoyed their five minutes with me before stamping me back into the country.

I arrived with the same beaten up suitcase and toolbox I had when I left and piling them onto a trolley I joined the queue at the taxi stand.

'Where to sir?' the taxi driver asked.

'The Southern Cross Hotel,' I told him with confidence.

In 1975 the Southern Cross in Collins Street was the best hotel in Melbourne where Frank Sinatra had recently stayed during his tour of Australia. If it's good enough for Frank its good enough for me, I thought.

It was late afternoon and raining when we pulled up outside the hotel. I left the luggage to the porters. Having struggled with my 36 kilo tool box half way around the world, I was more than glad to let somebody else carry it.

From the hotel I phoned Adam who was back in town having married Felicity and returned to Australia a few months ago. I met them in the *Hatter's Castle,* trendy pub on the corner of Punt Road and Toorak Road in South Yarra.

We spent a couple of hours in there catching up. Felicity was a breath of fresh air, her conversation lively and sharp, and I liked her immediately. When I told them where I was staying they couldn't believe my extravagance.

'Why, for Christ's sake? We have a spare bed.'

'Adam, it's for one night. I've never stayed in a five star pub and I want to get just a little taste of what it's like to have money.'

'Well if you keep staying there you won't have it for long,' Adam argued, his Scottish heart on his tartan sleeve.

They ran me back to the Southern Cross and came in for a drink with me in the bar. The concierge gave the three of us a bit of a doubtful look when we entered the building and tried to head us off before we got to the bar, but as soon as I produced my room key his demeanour softened. After a couple of drinks downstairs I took them up to show them my room. They were curious to see where Frank had stayed although somehow I couldn't help thinking Frank's room might have been a bit more upmarket than mine.

'I'll pick you up at 10 tomorrow, you're staying with us.' Adam told me in no uncertain terms, and that's what happened—but not before I'd enjoyed room service and breakfast in bed.

The next morning I gave the porter a $5 tip for putting my toolbox in the back of Adam's car, much to Adam's disgust.

'An hour's pay for a two second lift, you've got to be mental.'

We edged out into the light city traffic and headed out of Melbourne towards the Eastern Suburbs.

'I thought you lived in Elsternwick.'

'We do,' he said, 'but our first stop is a deceased estate in Kew.'

'Really?'

'Really. I feel there might be something a wee bit more rewarding on the horizon than being a maintenance fitter and this morning is a stepping stone towards that goal.'

'Tell me more.'

'Antique books,' he confided. 'There's a massive untapped market out there for a first print of *Treasure Island*, or *Moby Dick.*'

He proceeded to enlighten me on the antique books profession, his place in it, and its place in the world. By the time he'd finished I thought the grey monotony of a fitter's existence in a bleak Melbourne suburb was possibly preferable, but to each their own.

We found the address in Kew he was looking for, a big two-storey Victorian house that would be worth a pile in a few years. The woman who answered the door looked like she had been born before the house was built. She invited us in and Adam went into antique bookworm mode.

We were there to pick up a couple of hundred books that Felicity had eyeballed a few days earlier and there was also a bookcase to look at. We ferried the books out to Adam's station wagon until the back of the car was noticeably weighed down.

'There are some more in the library,' the old lady told us.

She led us down the hall into what had once been the library where we found four magnificent old empty bookcases, probably antiques. One of them looked fantastic. It stood almost eight feet high—double fronted with four glass doors on the top cupboard and wooden panelled doors on the bottom. The most striking feature of all was the carved front pediment, a work of art even to my untrained eye.

'This is made in one piece,' the woman informed us, 'and as I told Felicity, if you can get it out you can have it. The others are in sections so I can have them dismantled and sell them, but this one must have had the house built around it.'

There were half a dozen more boxes of books on the

floor and Adam said he would have to come back.

'That bookcase is not made in one piece,' I told Adam when we went outside.

'Tell me something I don't know. Let's get this lot home and see if we can get a truck.'

'Bring Felicity back.' I suggested. 'Get her to make the old girl a cup of tea and keep her talking while you and I take the thing apart.'

It was mid-afternoon when we returned with a box truck Adam had rented, plus Felicity armed with a packet of shortcake biscuits. How could this fail?

Felicity went on the attack while Adam and I climbed all over the bookcase looking for any hint as to how to take it apart. It took us about an hour to get the heavily carved top pediment off.

'If we get this outside, reassemble it and tell the old dear it was in one piece is she really going to give it to you?'

'Let's just get it apart and then see what she says.'

The bookcase was bloody heavy. I had no idea how we were going to load it into the truck, but as Felicity continued to keep the old lady occupied Adam and I continued to struggle. Once the pediment was removed, the bookcase developed a life of its own. The doors swung open making what was already a difficult job, a pretty dangerous one. We finally managed to dismantle the thing. Now all we had to do was get it outside and reassemble the parts. Piece of cake!

We were both fairly fit, but I wouldn't want to do this sort of hard yakka every day. Once we got the four pieces out onto the street we were able to reassemble the bookcase in the back of the truck. It was getting dark and cold when we eventually finished, but I was sweating.

We joined the two women back in the house.

'All done,' Adam told them.

'You've got it out?' the old lady asked. 'That's good.'

She directed us to the upstairs back bedroom so we could collect the remaining books. The bedroom was an

Aladdin's cave. Not only did we find the books but also several Hornby Double O train sets. I grew up with these things so I knew these were classics. The Sir Nigel Gresley Set, The Bristol Castle Set, The Mallard Set were all brand new and still in their boxes. A fourth box contained all the accessories—track and points, buildings, platforms—everything to set my heart racing.

The two women walked in as we were about to pick up the boxes of books.

'Are these train sets for sale?' I asked.

'Of course, I'll be glad to see the back of them. My husband loved trains, but in the end he bought more than he could ever use. The top box is something quite special really. Tom, my husband, worked with Nigel Gresley between the wars—they were both railway men.'

To call Sir Nigel Gresley a railway man was a bit like calling Neil Armstrong a bit of a flier. He was one of the main steam train designers in The Golden Age of Steam between the wars.

'How much do you want for the lot? I asked sheepishly.

She shook her head, 'I don't know.' Sitting down, she seemed suddenly tired of going over the same old ground.

'I'll be 86 in a couple of weeks and I have more money than I will ever need to see me through the rest of my life. My family will inherit everything—my useless son and his family of crows and vultures.' Her husband's bookcases and the train sets might be worth a thousand dollars, she explained, but to her they were worthless.

'I can see you have laboured hard to trick me into believing the bookcase was in one piece, so there is an obvious value in it for you. I can assume it is going to a good home where it will be admired for the fine piece of furniture it is. You are not going to sell it for a quick profit I hope?'

'No, no. We are opening an antique bookshop and this will be one of our centre pieces,' Felicity explained effortlessly.

'Take them. Take the train sets and take the bookcase.

My only stipulation is that you don't sell them but give them to people like yourselves who will enjoy them for what they are. Do we have a deal?'

Felicity shook her hand agreeing for the three of us.

We finally finished that night at close to ten o'clock having taken the bookcase apart again and stored it in pieces in their garage in Clarence Street. Then we took the truck back, just managing to grab a beer before closing time in the Elsternwick Hotel.

Adam bought the beer. 'Cheers,' he said as he handed me a glass, 'not a bad day's work.'

I nodded. 'We'd make quite a bit if we could turn a profit but we can't so ...' and I let it run away.

We sat in silence for a second or two.

'What do you have planned now?' Adam asked.

'First thing Monday I want to get a car. I think I've got a start up in Queensland. Need to make a couple of phone calls to confirm a few things, but that's probably where I'm headed. I've got a bit of money burning a hole in my pocket, so I'm looking at buying something, a flat, as an investment.'

'What about Kathy?' He asked.

'Nah, she's found someone else.'

I wasn't bitter. You can't do what I've been doing and expect to maintain a love life.

'It's going to be a busy few days, but I've got something even more pressing.'

'Oh aye, and what's that then?'

'I've got to find somewhere to set up me train set.'

50

My dad the airman

—ဆာ⍰—

The Germans, the Luftwaffe mainly, continued to give my dad a hard time. First of all it was his home that was flattened, then his sister's place just before Christmas. After that they seemed to bomb wherever he was working. No sooner had a ship been refitted than it was hit and sent to the bottom of the Thames. This was happening with monotonous regularity and it wasn't just the ship that went down but Dad's tools as well.

He was an apprentice and in those days apprentices bought their own tools. Losing them just didn't happen. If it happened once it was considered unfortunate, twice was downright careless, three times, well ....

Three of the ships my dad worked on never got out of the Port of London and he began to wonder if he was a jinx or a Jonah. The union gave him another tool box and told him to be careful where he left it so he took it everywhere he went!

As soon as he finished his apprenticeship, on his 21st

birthday, he went to enlist in the Royal Air Force. He could have stayed behind in a reserved occupation, but after three years on the receiving end of havoc wrought by German bombs, he wanted to give some back.

Because of his trade he became part of the ground crew repairing and patching up bombers. He worked at one of England's biggest air force bases in East Kirby, Lincolnshire, where, he said, the planes came back in 'shit condition'.

How the planes remained in the air was a compliment to their crews, especially the pilots, and the remains of a gunner from the tail turret would sometimes have to be hosed out before my dad could begin repairs.

Those working on the ground operated around the clock like a permanent pit crew. One morning, a flight returned followed back by a German Junkers 88 that strafed the air field, bombed the runway and shot up the mess. The old man wasn't impressed. He started to make plans to enlist in the aircrew.

At about this time a number of Polish airmen arrived who had escaped from Germany and joined the Free Polish Air Force. Most became part of a fighter squadron while the remainder were recruited to Bomber Command. My dad happened to be in their ranks during selection. The Poles were having trouble understanding orders and when one of them raised his hand to complain about this the sergeant told all the Poles to fall out. Not one to miss an opportunity Tom Garner fell out with them and became known as Tomski for the rest of the war.

Dad had worn glasses for most of his life and realised he couldn't meet the 20/20 vision requirement for joining the aircrew. Undeterred, he managed to get the eye test card from a nurse he was dating and learned it by heart. When the day of his medical came around he was given a clean bill of health. All that remained was the eye test.

'Can you read the bottom line?' the doctor asked him.

The letters were CZYL, which happened to spell a

Polish name. After weeks of rubbing shoulders with the Free
Polish Air Force, the old man quipped,

'C-Z-Y-L ... Read it? I know him!'

And that was how my dad joined Bomber Command.

I didn't know much about my dad's days as an airman.
Like most men of his generation he kept that part of his life
pretty much to himself. I've often wondered how I would
have coped with the stress of the daily and nightly routine he
had to deal with.

People who know both of us say that we are very
similar in our make-up and sense of humour. I like to think I
would have handled the war in the same manner he did. Yet
this is a massive presumption on my part. I have no idea how
you would wake up at about four o'clock in the afternoon to
prepare for another trip to Berlin or Dresden, never knowing
if you would be coming back.

If you were killed during the night it wouldn't be a
painless end either. You could expect to be burned to death
or to fall thousands of feet to be splattered over some foreign
field. Even if you escaped the burning wreck you could be
chopped up by the locals waiting for you when you floated
down on the end of your parachute.

I don't know how my dad prepared himself for that.
Perhaps you don't. Perhaps you just get on with it and hope
for the best.

I know he flew to Dresden. He told me that all they
took with them were oxygen bottles, five tons of them, to fuel
the fire they'd started the night before. I also know that he
flew to Düsseldorf.

A few years ago when I was working as a barman in
Spain, my dad turned up out of the blue with a few of his
mates. It was a busy Saturday night in Lloret de Mar with
customers six deep at the bar, and I waved excitedly as he
slowly made his way through the crowd. When a big blonde
bloke pushed in front of him, my old man, never one to be
backward in coming forward, dug his finger into the big

bloke's back.

'Oi, there's a queue here.' I heard my dad tell him.

The bloke gave my dad a mouthful in German which enraged the old man even more.

'Eric, where're you from?' the old man asked above the noise.'

'Düsseldorf.'

'Me, 1944 Lancaster bomber,' said my dad blowing a big raspberry and making a gesture with his hand to show what he'd done to Düsseldorf.

The German guy pushed my dad and the old man responded by head butting him which sparked a mini riot.

'Cheers Dad.'

Afterwards when the smoke had cleared I had a drink with him and his mates.

'I never knew that you went to Düsseldorf Dad.'

'There are a lot of things you don't know son.'

And that was so true. I would like to have got a lot closer to him, but it's not until it's too late that you feel like that. Right now I have a hundred questions for him. I know some of the answers and reading between the lines I think he had a good war. Still, what do I know?

—৪০০৪—

51

Books, borzois and train sets

The trouble with contracting is you never know when the next job is going to come along so you're afraid to spend. But once I found out I had a job starting in a couple of weeks up in Charters Towers I knew I could spend a little and I bought a 69 XW Falcon in good shape. I was told that the job was due to start in September, which gave me about three weeks to find an investment, buy a car and make my way up to Charters Towers.

While I was doing all that I also became briefly involved in the arty farty world of antique books, dog shows, and the very interesting Ms Leigh Barrington. The first time I met Leigh I'm not sure that she caught me in the right light. Adam and I were setting up the train set in the spare room and I must have looked every inch the anorak.

For some reason, when playing with trains, I always adopt a Yorkshire accent. I think Leigh caught me in mid 'EEEOOP Lad' wearing a station master's cap I bought at a Sunday market. Oh yeah, I could see she was impressed when Felicity introduced us.

The weekend before I was due to leave Adam and

Felicity took an exhibition stand at the annual Melbourne
Antiquarian Book Faire and the three of us spent most of
Friday shuttling back and forth from Elsternwick to St Kilda
Pavilion where the event was being held. They had quite a big
area for their display—even enough room to feature the new
bookcase. Adam and I had both become quite skilled in
assembling and dismantling this thing so it seemed a waste
not to use it. Despite the fact that I was starting to develop
muscles I never knew I had, although the time involved
turned out to be time well spent.

As we put the final touches to the display Felicity was
in her element, exchanging gems of chit-chat while dusting
books and introducing me.

'Larry this is Ken, this is Gaston, Larry this is Peter, this
is Kay.'

I imagined it would have been extremely difficult to
manage such an event on your own, as there seemed to be so
many aspects to attend to, setting up your stand was only a
part of it. Adam and I dealt with the menial stuff while Fiona
handled the public relations.

'Larry this is Leigh.'

'We've met,' Leigh said before Felicity could complete
the introduction. 'Not playing with your train set this evening?'
she asked, making sure everyone heard.

She caught me totally off guard and try as I might I
couldn't think of a witty or clever reply but her comment
brought life back into the flagging conversation especially
among the men. 'You have a train set?' someone asked.

I chuckled to myself. I think men of all ages and all
walks of life enjoy the idea of having a train set quietly stashed
away. I smiled at Leigh. 'You'll keep,' I thought.

On Saturday Adam and Felicity attended the faire
while I worked on my new car. I had a long drive ahead and I
wasn't going to be able to get the gear that was available in
Melbourne. I was just about finished, when I sensed I was
being watched. I smelt her before I saw her. Not having been

around women very much for the last year I found the subtle hint of perfume worked on me like a rat-trap.

'I like men who are good with their hands.'

'I'm pretty handy with my feet too.' I countered.

'What about other appendages?'

'I'm not really the person to ask there am I? But complaints are few and far between.' This was mainly because there hadn't been anybody for quite a while.

Leigh smiled. She was an attractive well-dressed woman in her late twenties with dark hair.

'I thought you would be at the Faire.' I said as I wiped my hands.

'I should be, but I needed to talk to you ...' she let it roll.

'What are you doing tomorrow?' she asked.

'Sunday? Church.'

'Somehow I don't think so.'

'What do you have in mind?'

'I have to attend a dog show in Croydon. I have borzois.'

'Must be painful.'

She smiled coldly.

'OK. What time?'

'We have to be there at ten.'

'So we leave here at ....'

'Well I was hoping that you could stay at my place tonight. Didn't Felicity tell you I'm having a little party?'

'No.'

I had been to sheep dog trials before but this was my introduction to the bitchy world of dog shows. The show in Croydon was a members' competition aimed at introducing people to showing dogs, how to train and groom them and how to handle them in preparation for the real thing.

But the event wasn't without its prima donnas. Leigh, not unlike Felicity yesterday, seemed to know almost everyone there, probably because she was president of the Victoria Borzoi Association. Borzois are a bit like Afghan or Irish wolfhounds—bloody big things. I learned that the two dogs being shown by Leigh were half hound and half Clydesdale, but I didn't know the breed was also very skittish.

There were other breeds at the show, all from different clubs and associations, and the members involved shared a common goal of trying to consume as much wine as possible before the end of the afternoon. As Leigh walked around with a glass the size of a goldfish bowl permanently half full, I obligingly kept her company.

By mid-afternoon I was quite hammered, which was ironic really: just when I felt like curling up for the remainder of the day it was time to show Leigh's two dogs. I had bought a new pair of work boots during the week thinking that the dog show would be a good place to break them in. There had been a bit of rain during the night and the boots were soon sodden and softening up nicely. I had both hounds on a leash, one in each hand as I prepared to walk them down the end of the arena and trot back with them as Leigh had instructed.

It seemed like a reasonable request. The dogs had been well trained, I was told, and would fall in with my stride as they passed the audience. There was no indication of any imminent danger as I walked them down to the end of the arena. Then everything went pear-shaped. As soon as I turned around and began to trot, my size 13 boots made a heavy thud that scared the dogs. They started running faster and I started running faster. Although at first I thought I could keep up with them it very quickly became apparent that they were going to beat me over the first hundred metres.

By the time we flew past the startled audience my feet were barely touching the ground and when they did come down they did so very loudly, causing the dogs to sprint even faster. Towards the end I was skimming across the ground, briefly touching down about every 20 feet or so, until I finally had to let go. The last time I saw the dogs they were heading for the Dandenong's.

That was the end of me and Leigh. It was short, but quite memorable.

❧

I bought number 15 Mansfield Street, Thornbury, the day before I left Melbourne. I was in two minds about it, but in the end the investment in the single bedroom unit proved to be possibly one of the smartest things I've ever done. I put down a ten grand deposit and never saw the place again, leaving the transaction in the capable hands of a friend of a friend who had recently graduated from university as a chartered accountant. He handled everything including the legal side and charged me next to nothing, just pleased to get his foot in the door.

So that was it, I spent my last night in Melbourne boxing up the train set. Adam and Felicity were going to be moving as well, now that their lease was coming to an end, so the last thing they needed was more stuff of mine to look after.

In another world and another time I would have loved setting up the train set, but for the time being I had to put away childish things. I loaded the four boxes into the back of the ute and drove over to Royal Children's Hospital on Flemington Road where I approached a male nurse on duty in reception.

'Can I help you?' he asked.

'Would you like a train set?'

'Pardon?'

'A train set, Hornby Double O.'

'Dr Alexander, this man wants to give us a train set.'

'Four actually,' I corrected.

The janitor was called and before I knew where I was I was handing the boxes to four very excited men who were really were old enough to know better.

I was asked to take the boxes up to the third floor and before I knew it half a dozen doctors, male nurses, a variety of hospital officials and a couple of visitors were discussing how and where to set it up. I hope the sick kids got to enjoy it, but I had a feeling the big kids were going to be playing with it for a while.

52

Lazza the Valiant

I had never fired a gun in my life. When I was growing up in London no-one I knew had one. I had fired a pellet gun in a fairground a couple of times, but I didn't really feel that counted. I told Nifty this once as we were drinking in the cricket club on Bougainville Island and he shook his head sadly.

'When you get back home, come up to Broken Hill. I'll take you out roo shooting Lazza, and teach you how to handle a gun.' Nifty seemed genuinely concerned that part of my education was sadly missing.

We had both returned from New Guinea to Australia at about the same time. I'd headed back to Melbourne while Nifty had returned to his home in Broken Hill, a mining town on the edge of the New South Wales outback.

After I decided to drive up to Queensland from Melbourne to take up my new job with a construction company, I gave Nifty a call. I told him I was heading north and that if he was home I'd take him up on his offer to teach me to shoot.

'My oath Lazza, get yer arse up here!' Nifty replied, which I assumed meant he'd be pleased to see me.

I left Melbourne early on the Saturday morning and drove into Broken Hill at just after four. Nifty, as promised, was propping up the bar at the Exchange Hotel on Argent Street. He looked like he might have been there for a few hours and he was holding court in much the same way he had done in the various bars in Bougainville.

Nifty was a big man, well over six feet tall, with a full head of sandy coloured hair and a permanent two day red growth that gave him a ruddy outdoor appearance. Since his younger days playing football most of the muscle he had put on was slowly softening but I reckoned he could still be a handful. Certainly he was a funny bugger who never let the truth ruin a good story.

As I walked into the bar he greeted me like a long lost brother. 'Lazza!' He bellowed getting the attention of the entire bar, and I immediately got the impression that if I was a friend of his I would be most welcome. Joining the throng sitting in a horseshoe around the bar I was introduced to Robbo, Davo, Johno, Big Davo and Muzza. I bought a round and settled into the group until it soon felt like I'd never been anywhere else.

Nifty and most of his mates were Eastern Suburbs football supporters so when the Easts' game was due to start we left the pub for Robbo's place to watch it on his telly. Nifty had told me in Bougainville that he'd been selected for a run out with Easts under 19s, but his mates, all of whom had known him for most of his life, couldn't remember exactly when this had happened. Anyway Easts ended up thumping the hapless Sea Eagles leaving the boys convinced that the team was heading for another premiership.

After the game, at about ten, Nifty, Robbo, Muzza and myself jumped back into my ute and headed out of town to Nifty's place.

'This is me country retreat Lazza. I've got a place in town, but on a weekend the boys and me like to come out here to relax.'

Christ, I thought, how much more relaxed could he get? After about 15 minutes we needed a piss break. We stopped the car and took a beer each.

'It's as black as a dog's guts out here Lazza, and look at them stars,' Nifty said, gazing up as he pissed on my leg. I looked up to see a billion gems twinkling back at us.

Then, true to form, Nifty had a tale to tell. 'Just before you arrived in the pub today a bloke came in, very distraught. "Give me a glass of your best whiskey," he told Maureen the barmaid. "Better make it a double," he added, and Maureen repeated the measure. He skulled it, demanded more, and Maureen obliged with another double *Chivas*. "Blimey mate", I said, "I've never seen a bloke drink top shelf whiskey like you before." "You do that when you've got what I've got," he replied. "And what's that?" I asked. The bloke laughed. "Sixty eight cents!"'

We burst out laughing. Then we each opened another can, got back in the car, and continued on our way.

After one more piss stop we made it to Nifty's country estate. 'Me old man bought this place just after the war,' Nifty explained. 'He and his brother and another couple of blokes all put in a few bob and over the years we've added to it. Maybe it ain't the flashiest place in the world but I like it.'

It was dark, so I took his word for it. We unloaded our supplies which consisted of half a dozen cartons and went in. There was a big open fireplace with a pile of logs in the hearth and the whole of the inside of the house—surprisingly clean and tidy—was open so that it was difficult to see where the kitchen started and the lounge ended.

Another couple of beers later, the boys were ready to go shooting. They had 'modified' an old Toyota Land Cruiser for the purpose, a vehicle that bore the scars of many previous expeditions like the one we were about to embark upon.

Nifty took the wheel while Robbo acted as 'spotter' from the passenger seat and Muzza and I stood in the back. There seemed to be guns everywhere!

We must have driven nearly 100 kilometres over some extremely dark, rough country. Muzza and I were nearly thrown into oblivion on at least a dozen occasions, and at least another carton of *Tooheys* was consumed. I was surprised that we only got bogged once. But as the morning sun started to brush the Eastern horizon it became clear that the kangaroo population of this part of New South Wales could rest easy for another day.

Not to have sighted a single roo was very rare and we sat on the back of the truck pondering the night's events. Then, just as Nifty was about to accuse me of putting a jinx on the expedition, a wild pig suddenly appeared from nowhere.

'Holy shit Lazza, look what we have here.' Nifty pulled his lever action 22 Winchester from its sheath, put a bullet in the chamber and he handed it to me. Uncertain, but not wanting to look like a complete tool, I took careful aim, slowly squeezed the trigger and a spurt of blood burst from the pig's head. It went down without a twitch: I had shot it dead right between the eyes.

'Holy shit Lazza,' Nifty said again, 'that shot must have been 50 or 60 meters.' He was impressed but I wasn't. I'd caught and eaten a few fish but this was the first animal I had ever killed. Killing a pig simply because I was expected to didn't really make me feel very good, and not for the first time I knew I'd never become a great white hunter.

After a little ceremony in which I was smeared with a bit of blood we drank the last of the beer and headed back to town.

By the time we returned to Nifty's place, the sun was up, and I got a look at his country estate for the first time in daylight. There had obviously been no covenant or building permission required as it seemed to have been built to no standard whatsoever. Steel, timber, brick and almost any building material that was handy had been used. Still, I had to admit, it did have a rustic charm and I could understand why it would have appealed to Nifty.

'I'm going to render the whole thing one day,' he said as if reading my mind.

'Yeah that'll fix it.' I lied.

Once I had showered and changed, Nifty and I set off back into town. Muzza had already gone to bed, and Robbo looked like he wouldn't be far behind. The sun had been up for a couple of hours, it was only just after seven and already there was a bite to it.

We were still on the dirt about thirty k's out of town when we spotted a car broken down on the side of the road. There seemed to be a lot of people milling around so Nifty's first reaction was to keep going.

'It'll be Abbos Laz. They know how to look after 'emselves: don't stop.'

As we approached however I was surprised by Nifty's change of tack.

'Wow, 'ang on mate, that's Thommo's sister and that's Davo's brother's Valiant.'

Of course it was. We stopped across the road from about five or six youngsters and an old R Model Valiant that looked like it had been lovingly restored. Nifty got out and everyone seemed to know him.

'What's the problem?' he wanted to know.

'It just stopped,' someone said.

Nifty looked under the bonnet, but after a few minutes he gave up. 'You've got fuel,' he said, 'but no spark, could be any number of things and I need a few tools to tell you what it is. Come on, we'll give you a tow back into town.'

He turned to me and said, 'This might be alright, I'm jumping in with Sharon, she's not a bad sort, and Carol can get in with you. You'll like Carol.' And with that he scarpered.

I reversed the Falcon around until I was in front of the Valiant. Judging from the decent rope that was pulled from the boot, it seemed like this might have happened before. I've always found that people who live in the bush do travel with everything, prepared for the worst on the long lonely roads.

We hooked up the cars and people jumped in the Valiant, leaving Carol, an attractive young woman of about 19, looking a bit lost.

'Jump in with me,' I suggested and she did. The rest is history.

I took up the strain and pulled away. The Falcon hardly noticed the added weight, and I accelerated up to about 35k's an hour. That was fast enough on the dirt road I thought.

I glanced across at Carol. She had shoulder-length dark hair, brown eyes and delicate facial features and was wearing a denim shirt with pop-fasteners, open low enough to allow me a good glimpse of her firm young breasts. My eyes returned to the road but, almost like a magnet, they were drawn back to the objects of my fascination.

'D'you like 'em? She had caught me in mid-ogle.

'Absolutely!' I replied, stating the obvious.

Then an amazing thing happened. She popped open the front of her shirt, and as my foot sat a little heavier on the accelerator, unclipped the front of her bra to completely reveal her two perfect breasts.

I was now kind of flummoxed; what was I to do? As if reading my mind she completely unflummoxed me. Her head dived into my lap like a compass to north, she fumbled with my zipper and in a few seconds she was working away on me.

She was obviously used to attending to blokes from Broken Hill, and she persevered until she got results. 'HO, HO!' I said, or something similar. She really started to enjoy herself and I wasn't having a bad time either. I'd been drinking for about 13 hours and whether it was because of this or the complete surprise, I seemed to have a lot more staying power than usual.

'Yes … yes …. OH YES!' I yelled, banging on the steering wheel, my foot hard down on the accelerator pedal. I closed my eyes briefly during the magic moment then looked down at the speedo. I was doing 174 kilometres per hour!

I quickly glanced up to the mirror and I couldn't believe my eyes. Through the dust the front of Valiant emerged completely sand blasted, with not a speck of yellow paint to be seen. The headlights were gone, the windscreen was gone, the radiator grill was gone, the chrome trim and mirrors were all gone, and Nifty was on the bonnet being held by his boots while trying to cut the tow rope with his penknife!

'OH NO!' I shouted.

I slowed down, pulled over to the side of the road and came to a stop as Nifty slid off the bonnet of the Valiant and landed in a heap in the dust.

'YOU STUPID POMMY BAAAS ...' he yelled as he chased me around my car but he stopped when he saw the front of the Valiant for the first time.

'I don't believe it!' he cried and then started to laugh as he took in the sight of the car and the six shell shocked people inside 'Has anyone got a camera?'

'I have,' said Carol meekly, probably aware that this had all been her fault.

Nifty took photos of the stunned crew in the car. Then someone took one of Nifty and me hamming it up in front of sandblasted Valiant with Nifty's arm wrapped around my neck and his massive fist in my face.

'Hell Lazza, that was bloody interesting,' he observed with typical understatement.

After a few minutes, when the dust had literally settled, we decided to continue into town. Carol directed me to the home of the owner of the Valiant and six of us pushed it up the drive. We left it with the rear of the car facing the front door so there was no indication of the carnage at the front. I would love to have been a fly on the fence when Davo's brother, whoever he was, discovered that a bit of body work might be in order.

'Maybe he won't notice,' Nifty suggested as we drove off.

I dropped him off outside the Exchange Hotel. 'You coming in for one?' he asked.

I declined as I knew one with Nifty would very quickly become two. 'No thanks mate, I've got to be heading off.'

We shook hands and he walked into the bar. 'You'll never guess what just happened,' I heard him say to someone as I drove away.

I'd like to say that Nifty and I had a few more adventures over the years that followed but sadly that was the last time I ever saw him. I spent the next twenty years travelling around Australia and overseas before returning with my family to Queensland. I phoned Nifty a couple of times and we both promised to catch up, but it never happened. Then in 2004 I received word to say he was sick and he wanted to see me. Unfortunately I was in Laos working, and a fortnight later came the news that he had died.

I flew to Adelaide the next day and drove out to Broken Hill in time for the funeral. The church was full to overflowing. It seemed most of Broken Hill had turned up to say goodbye.

The wake was held as expected at the Exchange Hotel and it was there that I finally met Sharon, Nifty's girlfriend. She turned out to be the same Sharon who Nifty had latched onto that Sunday morning nearly 30 years ago. Like all wakes it was a bit stiff at first, but the alcohol loosened everyone up, and it became as pleasant as those occasions can be. At about six o'clock I decided it was time to make tracks and I looked for Sharon to say goodbye.

'Don't leave just yet Laz, I have a couple of things to show you.' Sharon looped her arm through mine as we walked the short distance to the home that she had shared with Nifty.

'Whatever happened to the "country estate"?' I asked.

She laughed. 'When they built the road out to Menindee Lake it ran right past the front of it. The council told them to either fix up the house or tear it down. They did neither and eventually the council bought it. Nifty got quite a bit for it but he either drank it or gambled it all away,' she said sadly.

When we got to her home she showed me into a large living room at the back with various pictures on the wall. There in the centre of the sideboard was the framed photo of Nifty and me, the one taken all those years ago in front of the sandblasted Valiant.

'You wouldn't believe how many times he told that story,' Sharon said smiling, 'and every time it was funnier than the last.'

I picked it up and looked at the two of us. The photo had faded slightly but the camera had caught both of us perfectly.

'I've got a few miles out of it too.' I confessed, returning the picture to its pride of place.

'Come on,' she said, 'I've got something else to show you.' She produced a key from her pocket and unlocked an old wooden garage at the back of the house. We dragged open the double doors, flicked a switch and there under the lights gleamed a 1962 R Series Valiant.

'Is this the same car?' I asked, knowing the answer.

She nodded. 'Nifty bought it off Thommo, not long after, for a couple of hundred bucks and spent years restoring it.'

I ran my fingers over the highly polished bonnet—the car was in immaculate condition both inside and out. I stood back to admire its classic lines when I noticed the registration plate, 'Lazza'!

Sharon saw that I noticed. 'In Broken Hill, Lazza, you are almost royalty!'

53

Dirt roads, wild places

You don't really get a feel for how big Australia is until you drive it. When I drove the 1765 kilometres from Perth to Port Hedland it seemed like massive distance, especially as my dad had me trained to rotate the tyres before we went on any long journey. A long journey to him was 85 miles, but most of the Aussies I met thought nothing of driving home to Perth, and were often tempted to nip home if we went out on strike.

The joy, if there is such a thing, of driving that road is that there are frequent places to stop such as Karratha, Carnarvon and Geraldton, but when I checked the map after leaving Nifty's place in Broken Hill I couldn't see any likely stopovers until I got to Milparinka, which was 400 kilometres of dirt away. Still, for a dirt road this one was in excellent condition, and I was able to cover the distance in under five hours—just before I ran out of fuel.

I've always been impressed by what people from the bush carry in their cars. If you live out there you need everything, water being the first requisite, fuel coming a close

second, and key engine parts such as hoses, belts and plugs.
I should have learned my lesson in Western Australia but
I hadn't, so this led to a very anxious last hour or so. I arrived
in Milparinka with less than zero in the tank, really pleased to
see the sign telling me I'd made it. Even so, apart from the
sign and the gas station, there was precious little else there,
not even a pub.

At Tibooburra half an hour further down the road,
I arrived just in time to miss lunch, so I topped up with fuel
again and bought two jerry cans. I thought the cans might
cost me an arm and a leg, but ten bucks each seemed not a
bad price out here. It was a very lonely, wild and windswept
place, close to the point where New South Wales, Queensland
and South Australia meet. Much as I would have liked to have
stood on that spot I was told I'd have needed a four wheel
drive and a guide to find it and I was keener still to put some
more miles behind me.

Continuing along the Silver City Highway I made it to
the border, a desolate windy area with nothing as far as the
eye could see. I stopped and walked a bit to stretch my legs,
thinking how I loved this wild place but how its remoteness
also scared me. Break down out here and it could be a long
time before someone came along. Yet no sooner had this
thought crossed my mind, than I saw a road train coming
towards me. The vehicle slowed and finally came to a stop.

'You right?' the driver asked.

'I'm fine, just stretching my legs.'

'Where are you headed?'

'Charters Towers.'

'You've got a long way to go.'

'Yeah, I wanted to get to Quilpie tonight but that's not
going to happen.'

'You should make Nock by dark,' he told me.

'Anything there?'

He shook his head. 'No, not really.'

'Where're you headed?'

'Adelaide ... be in Broken Hill tonight, Adelaide tomorrow mid-day.'

'Good Luck,' I said, 'and thanks for stopping.'

'No worries.'

He waved as he went on his way and the silence descended again.

I reached Nockatunga just as the light was starting to fade. Because these back routes could be dangerous at night with kangaroos, brumbies and scrub turkeys in the road, I made up my mind when I was talking to the truck driver that I would sleep in the back of the ute tonight. I had a few things in the esky other than half a carton of VB; not much, but enough to cook a good meal. I pulled off the road to a spot behind some trees and made camp.

After starting a fire, I boiled some water, made tea and toasted some bread, then warmed some beans and fried a couple of pieces of bacon. It was nothing flash but I liked it, and there was no-one else to please.

I left at first light aiming to get to Barcaldine by nightfall. Just before Quilpie I shredded a tyre and although I had a spare, I needed more than one on these roads. Once I arrived in Quilpie I bought a couple of recaps (re-treads), which were all I could afford, and I also replaced the air filter.

I'd thought of stopping in Blackall, my next port of call, but it's true what they say about the place, so after refuelling I was quickly back on the bitumen heading for Barcaldine. That's where I found a motel, enjoyed a good soak, downed a couple of beers and ate a beautiful steak in the little pub on the corner.

I met a bloke in the bar who'd never left Barcaldine.

Don't you think you're missing something?' I asked.

'Nope. Sooner or later almost everyone passes through here.'

After a short pause he looked at me. 'Where're you from?'

'London.' I told him.

'See, you're here.'

'Well there's no denying that.'

I was back on the dirt again the next day covering the 300 kilometres from Barcaldine to Aramac and then up to the Pentland. I limped into Torrens Creek with another shredded tyre and the other recap in poor shape. Unfortunately I didn't have a credit card—I was down to my last 50 bucks—but I managed to find another recap. It wasn't much better than the one I already had. Still, it got me to Charters Towers.

I had left Broken Hill on Monday morning at about eight and by four on the Wednesday afternoon I'd covered almost exactly the same distance as the coast road route from Perth to Port Hedland. This was a big country and I was getting to see quite a bit of it.

54

Charters Towers

The Paisley brothers, Jim and Bill, were staying at the Crown Hotel and had booked me into a room. They had won a contract to build a small gold-processing plant just outside town where the material was starting to arrive, but the workforce was yet to be seen. So I think they were as pleased to see me as I was to see them. At any rate, before the dust had settled they whisked me off to survey the site.

The mine, called Disraeli, was located about 15 miles down the Emerald Road. Civil construction was under way with bases and plinths being erected, and soon they would start to stand the structural steel and the steelwork that would be the skeleton of the plant.

'We've got a guy coming up from Melbourne who's going to put the mills together,' Jim told me, 'we'd like you to work with him.' Jim said one of the mills, from a mine down in Gympie had already arrived and was over in a paddock.

'Where's everyone else?' I asked.

'Coming, coming,' Bill assured me. 'There's not much we can do apart from prep work until the concrete is ready in a week or so, but don't worry we'll find plenty to keep you occupied.'

They certainly did. It was good to be working again and over the next few days more people turned up as the workload increased. A couple of cranes arrived from Townsville together with a crane truck and wobbly BHB crane that looked pre-war and possibly was. A week later we had about a dozen guys on the job.

Chris, Russ and I worked with Jeff, the guy formerly with Vickers in Melbourne. He now spent his time going around the world inspecting shagged out pieces of equipment and reporting on whether they still had any life left in them.

We spent the first couple of weeks cleaning the mill, removing the old grease, filing or grinding off burrs and bruises of which there were surprisingly few. These old machines were well engineered and if they were well maintained, as these big old machines obviously had been, they would give years more service.

'It might be a job in the bush, but it's not a bush job.' Jeff told me on more than one occasion.

Jeff was of the old school, pedantic and fastidious, a man who knew how to get what he wanted. He was my dad's age and I found a lot of other similarities between them: they both taught me a lot.

We got paid fortnightly and my first pay cheque was more than welcome. I had been living pretty frugally over the previous two weeks so it was nice to have a bit to spend at last.

Charters Towers was an old mining settlement that turned into a boom town when gold was first discovered around there in the late 19th century. The first stock exchange in Australia was established in Charters Towers, and at the height of the boom there were 104 pubs in the town. By the mid-1970s that number had dwindled, but there was still more than you could visit in one night.

Charters Tower, Broken Hill and Kalgoorlie, three towns scattered across Australia, were remarkably similar in many ways. Close your eyes turn around three times and it'll take you a few minutes to discover which one you are in. Each town had more pubs than they knew what to do with and each pub was unique.

The pubs generally sponsored footy clubs, associations going back in some cases to before WWI, so if you supported a certain team you drank at a certain pub. Most were museums as well as excellent watering holes.

We worked a 10-hour day. The beauty of construction work was that by six o'clock you were finished, with no call-outs, no breakdowns and a whole evening to enjoy. I became pretty good mates with Chris, a Vietnam Vet who looked and sounded much older than he really was, and with Russ who was in his mid-30s. They had both worked for Paisley Engineering on a number of occasions.

'I thought they'd dress up in paisley overalls, a bit like the circus,' Chris started to explain.

'The Circus?'

'World Services. You never worked for them?'

'No.'

'Melbourne outfit. They used to give us overalls with each panel a different colour. We looked like bloody clowns, hence the Circus.'

'Why? Why do that?' I asked.

'If they were doing a big shutdown at one of the refineries in Altona or Hastings where there were a number of contractors on site, they could see which men were theirs.'

'Bet the union loved that.'

'The union couldn't do much about it. The blokes never complained because the company paid over the going rate.'

I ordered another round and when the barman served me he offered us a proposition.

'You boys are going to be in town for a while aren't you?'

'I hope so,' I said, 'my account's a bit threadbare at the moment. Why?'

'You were asking how many pubs there are in town the

other night. Well, the Wheelbarrow Race is coming up and it'll give you a chance to sample all of them.'

'Tell me more.'

'A few years ago the nurses tried to raise some money for their kiddies' wing at the hospital. They came up with the idea of walking around town with a wheelbarrow and people threw their change into the barrow. Well, they figured they could raise money quicker if they had more than one barrow and that's how it became a race.'

The barman explained that every year more teams had become involved as it was for such a good cause and every pub now entered its own team.

'But we don't have a team in it yet,' he added, 'and we were hoping you'd run for us. You look like a fit bunch of lads.'

'How many in a team?'

'Four to six, with one person always in the barrow.'

I looked at Chris and Russ. They weren't so keen, but I knew who would be.

We had a rigger working with us, Little Pete, who stood about five feet six, weighed seven stone and would make an excellent jockey. Then there was Eamon, an Irish back packer Jim brought in one morning. He was strong as an ox and twice as bright, just the sort of lad who would be interested in such a venture. I wasn't sure who'd fill the other voids but I knew I'd find someone.

'Put us down and I'll give you the names later. When is it?

'Show Day, the last weekend in September.'

'We'll be there,' I told him excitedly.

55
The wheelbarrow race

At work the following morning, I had no trouble in rounding up the rest of the team. Eamon was all for it as I knew he would be and so was Pete. Jim and Bill got involved in designing the wheelbarrow. They bought one, covered it with their Paisley Brothers Construction logo and added wheels to the bottom of the stand. They also fitted a harness to the front and back of the wheelbarrow so it could be pulled as well as pushed.

We even put in some light training. I hadn't done any serious running since ... well I couldn't remember, and it showed. They had failed to tell us what the course was, and what the rules were, and while we were concentrating on getting fit we found that running was not involved after all. However, we were expected to drink a beer at every hotel along the route.

David, the manager of the Crown, had done the race a couple of times. He cautioned that it wasn't easy. 'Take your time—you won't do it in 10 minutes—some haven't completed it in 10 hours.'

The killer, Dave warned, was going out to St Pat's pub, which was about a kilometre away and a kilometre back. He explained that the race started at various venues at ten o'clock.

'You have to set off from your sponsored pub, in your case here, and this year you finish at the Court House Hotel. There are 13 pubs in the race—rather an ominous number.'

The whole town dressed up for show day, although the event really lasted three days in all. It started on the Thursday and finished on the Saturday evening with a dance that we were all looking forward to. It was business as usual for us, but we were all given the Saturday off, and in hindsight giving us Sunday as well might have been a good idea.

We started the race at the Crown on Mossman Street, having been given the official nod by Dave at exactly ten. Heeding our manager's advice we drank the first beer slowly before heading across the road to the Royal. We took our time at the Royal and enjoyed our second beer there while Pete collected a few pennies from the early drinkers and tourists. I'd been in Charters Towers three weeks so I considered myself a lifer rather than a tourist.

Our next stop was the Commercial Hotel and then the Waverley, where we had our first encounter with half a dozen nurses from Charters Towers Hospital. They were in the same mould as all the nurses I've ever met, lots of fun, sharp as razors and game for almost anything. They fell for Eamon's blarney, but then again so did I. We promised to see them later if we were still standing.

We finished off Mossman Street at the Parkview, meeting a team of rugby players who were almost as friendly as the nurses. What is it about country people? You always think that there's an ulterior motive behind their demeanour and it takes a long time before you realise they are just genuine, nice people. I hate that!

We had done all but two of the pubs on Mossman and were now about to tackle the six in Gill Street. The day was becoming fun. The White Horse was full of wheelbarrows and bonhomie as the beer began taking effect. Then I think we made for the Phoenix, although it was about there that things started to become a wee bit hazy.

We arrived at the Excelsior just in time to beat the nurses to the bar. They all fancied Eamon but Mick and I knew we could always pick up the crumbs. Story of my life. The Enterprise and the Sovereign came next, and then we headed down the road to St Pat's. We shouldn't have run, we really shouldn't, but we did.

In the short time we'd been in Charters Towers, St Pat's was probably the only pub I hadn't visited, and from what I can vaguely remember I liked it immediately. I was full of *joie de vivre*, as I usually am after 10 beers. Everyone looked very attractive and the nurses were there again. It would have been the easiest thing in the world to abandon the race, sit down on the grass in the beer garden and enjoy everyone's company, but surprisingly it was Eamon who burst the bubble and got us back on the road again.

We finished our beer in St Pat's and headed back up the hill into town, quickly followed by one of the many rugby teams in the race. Now we were walking rather than racing. While we'd had designs on winning, just finishing would be nice.

There were only two more pubs to go, the Rix and finally the Court House Hotel for the finish. We'd lost Mick who had probably stayed behind with the nurse he wanted to take out into the rose garden. We weren't going to win, but it didn't really matter. It had been an excellent day in any case.

We ambled up the hill to the Rix with me in the wheelbarrow, and were having one in there when word filtered through that there was still no-one at the Court House. The entire day was becoming very blurred. All I knew was that our race card had been stamped by every pub we'd visited and that we'd collected a wheelbarrow full of change.

Eamon was threatening to leave until I convinced him that we were in with a chance of winning this thing. Mick reappeared from his brief encounter, and Gary and Mick, the remaining members of our team, could barely stand, but we were all still intact.

We put Pete back in the barrow and set off down to the Court House about 50 metres away, managing to cross the road without mishap. Amazingly, we entered the Court House to a tumultuous reception. All that remained for us to do was drink just one more stubbie (375ml) and we had won. Our card was checked, our cash counted and it took us about 15 minutes to finish that last stubbie before being crowned official champions of the Charters Towers Wheelbarrow Race. Apparently the party that followed developed into quite a good night but god knows where I was. It was Tuesday before I recovered.

56

Serious engineering

In Charters Towers I was employed in my first construction job, building a small gold processing plant. Of all base and precious metals, gold is possibly the easiest to process. The ore passes through a series of crushers and then through a SAG (semi autogenous grinding) mill, which reduces it to a coarse gravel. Next the gravel is pulverised to a fine sand in a ball mill so that the gold is released from the rock, and the recovery process can begin. SAG and ball mills can best be described as very big tumble driers one-third full of hard iron grinding balls.

I had served a recognised apprenticeship as a maintenance fitter, but now I found myself learning a completely different set of skills. Wearing a pair of shorts and a T shirt, I was as far from the workshop in London where my basic training had started as I could get in every concept. I looked forward to every day.

Everything may have been new to me but the equipment we were working on was anything but. The two mills we were going to install had come from a redundant mine in Gympie, an old mining town in south east Queensland. Jeff and a small crew had meticulously taken the Gympie plant apart piece by piece and had painstakingly marked every item so that re-assembly would be as easy as possible.

Our site had already been levelled and over a thousand tons of concrete poured into pump bases, tank bases, bund walls and the massive plinths that were to hold the mills. The SAG mill was about 30 feet in diameter and about the same in length, while the ball mill was about 20 feet in diameter and 35 feet long. Each mill weighed over a hundred tons and had been shipped in about a dozen pieces. They were now in a neighbouring paddock awaiting some minor preparation before assembly could begin.

As soon as the concrete had cured, Jeff had me scabbling or roughing up the surface to prepare it for the grout. Then we tackled the large, heavy sub-sole plates, large heavy plates, positioning five of these plates on top of the first plinth, followed by another five on the second. These plates would form the base that the mills would eventually sit on.

As the sun sank behind the trees and we were packing our tools away, I knew this was something I had always wanted to do. It had been a gorgeous day, not too hot, but even if the mercury had hit a hundred I wouldn't have known, as I'd been so absorbed.

'Fancy a beer Larry?' Jeff asked.

'My oath,' I smiled as he handed me a cold can from the esky he had in the boot of his car. A beer never tasted better.

৵

The next morning we went out to the paddock where the SAG mill lay in three pieces. The fifty-ton shell sat in its cradle, while the two enormous end caps were lying on railway sleepers in the long grass. We spent the day cleaning the contacting faces until all the burrs, and blemishes were removed and the polished metal shone under the punishing sun. We went on to coat the faces with a light oil to prevent rust developing, and when Jeff was convinced that they were ready, we started to put the SAG mill back together.

It was a reasonably easy process of lifting each end cap with the crane, finding the match marks and bolting the caps to the shell. Even the 90 bolts and bolt holes had been individually numbered for easy assembly. We tightened the bolts but they would need to be torqued to the correct setting when we were finishing.

When we had completed the assembly of the SAG, we did the same with the ball mill. Although it was repetitious work, with nearly 30 tons dangling on the end of the crane hook, we gave the job the respect it deserved. By Saturday afternoon Jeff and Russell and I were just about finished, and I thought we might have had Sunday off but Jeff had other ideas.

The new white metal bearings still had to be scraped to fit—a monotonous but important job. It took Russ and me three days to achieve what Jeff wanted, which was 90 per cent contact between the bearing and the journal. We tried to cheat by applying too much Engineers Blue.

'Nice try lads,' laughed Jeff, 'it might be a job in the bush, Larry, but it isn't a bush job.'

So everything was meticulously measured and aligned, the sole plates installed and positioned, and finally the bearing housings were lowered on top of the sole plates.

'Just in time,' Jeff told us, 'we have the 250 arriving tomorrow morning.'

He had hired a 250 ton hydraulic crane out of Townsville to lift the two mills onto their bearing in the plant. The crane arrived during the night with its own fleet of trucks carrying the counterweights, rigging gear and its own crew of riggers.

In the morning we discussed the lift, making sure the riggers knew exactly what was required. They didn't come cheap, so we wanted to do the job once, do it properly, and send them back to Townsville as quickly as possible.

It was good working with these guys. This was serious, heavy engineering and I saw it as my future. Jeff had cut me enough slack, allowed me to take charge, and the riggers seemed pleased to work with me. I was only 25, but I like to think I had developed a confidence without the arrogance that I sometimes saw in project leaders, and over the years I have always tried to maintain that attitude.

We helped the riggers set up the crane and by mid-morning they were ready to lift the SAG Mill in its cradle onto the back of the lowboy truck, drive it down to the site and unload it.

The lift was over in just a few agonising minutes. I knew the measurements were right as I had repeatedly gone over every one, but I still wasn't convinced all would go well. So it was an extremely satisfying moment when I noticed the crane's chains slacken and finally saw the mill slightly rocking on its bearings.

Jeff saw how anxious I was. 'Happy now?' he asked.

I smiled but shook my head. 'Not until the ball mill is sitting down.'

&

The whole procedure was then repeated successfully with the ball mill. But there was no time to rest on our laurels. Still to come was the delicate and exacting job of fitting the drive train from the massive 2000 horsepower motor through the gear box to the ring gear, which was bolted to the shell of each mill. The gear was out in the paddock sitting on timbers, or dunage as they called it in Queensland.

Over the next few days Russ and I cleaned the teeth of the gear, removed the protective grease on it and touched it up with files and emery cloth. The two large 'C'-shaped segments that made up the large girth gear seemed in reasonable condition, but Jeff insisted that we touched up every tooth and removed anything that might interfere with its smooth performance. Once the gear and the machined bolts were cleaned up we installed the gear, first the SAG and then the ball mill. It was like a giant jigsaw puzzle and there was immense pleasure in watching all the pieces fit together.

❧

Over the next few days we had a number of new starters, including a lot of electricians.

'I hate sparkies,' said Ray, another new starter. 'We stand the steel, turn our backs and they're laying their cable trays in the rack where we've already run some pipe.' He was right of course and that is why over the years there has been a running battle between sparkies and the rest of the construction fraternity.

But I must admit these sparkies were different. They were from Darwin. I don't know why that should have made a difference, but their supervisor was a bloke called Pedro who I got on with like a house on fire. He asked me where we were up to with the pipe and what racks we wanted to use, a straightforward approach, which saved a lot of agro.

Years later, working on a job in the Northern Territory, I saw some work I recognised.

'Is Pedro here?' I asked.

'Not anymore,' I was told, 'but he was here.'

'I thought I recognised his signature.'

A better compliment I don't think I can give. Pedro was a quality tradesman and a good bloke—definitely wheelbarrow race material.

The sparkies, meanwhile, pulled their heavy electrical cables while we continued with the installation of the mills.

'The mill is fixed,' Jeff explained, 'so that is now our datum point. Always work from something that is fixed.'

Jeff had made everything about the job simple. At the start I'd had a hundred questions and he took the time to answer every one. Over the years I've always tried to have the patience to do the same.

After we fitted the girth gear we finally torqued up every bolt—a tedious, time-consuming operation. In Northern Queensland at the start of the summer the sun had a real bite to it and for Russ and I there was no escape from the relentless heat. We built makeshift tents and canopies, but nothing really worked so we came in late and worked through the night.

We then started to install the drive, fixing the pinion gear and pinion bearings before aligning the pinion to the girth gear. Jeff was insisting once again that there should be no compromise, and using Engineers Blue we managed to get the pinion and the girth gear as close to perfect as possible. We had previously installed the mills' lubrication systems, but because we had no power to run the pumps we used a manual jacking pump to lift each mill whenever we turned it. Slowly but surely the mills were coming together.

57

Sparkies meet their match

When Paisley Construction hired me and found out that I had a first aid certificate I became the official first aid attendant on site. I had taken my St John's First Aid Course in Bougainville and we'd staged a couple of mock accidents in the classroom for practice, but the setting was far from the real thing.

I have always believed that if you are going to become a qualified first aider you should spend a few hours in the casualty department of your local hospital to get used to seeing the type of accidents you might be dealing with on a regular basis. But I never did, so it was fortunate that all I was dealing with on site was a couple of nicks and cuts and the occasional case of sunburn. All that, however, was about to change.

The next day I was out in the paddock waiting to pick up one of the gearboxes, the boys were unloading the latest truck in from Gympie. Pete was driving the BHB Wobbly Crane while the truck driver was on the back of his vehicle 'slinging' the loads. Jim had learned about the price and lead time on new grid mesh steel and had told the people in

Gympie to send us whatever they had left and we'd make what we could out of that.

I was scouting around the paddock looking to see what else was left when I heard a horrible noise. The supply of grid mesh would have been awkward enough to unload at the best of times but it didn't seem to have been stacked properly on the truck. Almost inevitably, as soon as the men started to take it down, the steel slipped and a lot of it crashed off the truck, bringing the driver down with it and crushing his legs.

I was the first person on the scene, arriving there even before Pete could get out of the crane. I'd never seen a compound fracture until that moment and I was useful for the first few seconds. Then I saw the bone sticking through the truck driver's jeans and promptly crumpled into a heap. I called for assistance on the radio.

Jim answered straight away, 'What is it?'

'We've had an accident out in the paddock. Request immediate assistance, ambulance and two stretchers.'

'Two men down?'

'One down and the other stretcher is for me. I'm not going to go the distance!'

So much for my St John's certificate. I did manage to stay vertical until the ambulance arrived and was more than happy to let them take over. I don't do crushed limbs very well.

I could treat sunburn though. It was late spring and not only becoming hot out there, but the humidity was also starting to climb. In those days we spent most of the day dressed in just shorts and boots—even the hard hat wasn't mandatory—so that we'd forget just how fierce the sun was. Sunburn became almost an epidemic. All of us Anglos burned very quickly. We'd be kicked off site these days for even thinking about doing our jobs without protection. Shame really, because it was an excellent way to work.

Anyway, I digress. After the steel delivery, the gearbox was our next priority. We took that apart, fitted new bearings and while we had it stripped we drilled and tapped some holes in the base to help us with the alignment.

We found a small machine shop in town not far from the hospital and while we were in the area we called to see the injured truck driver. He had shattered his leg in three places but he was going to be OK. In fact when Eamon and I saw him he was pretty well doped up on morphine and feeling quite pleased with the world. So was Eamon. Instead of working with me as he was supposed to, he was renewing his relationship with the nurses. He looked a bit like Steve McQueen, which helped I suppose. I sat there one morning trying to listen to his patter, but although he could be quite charming he never really had any. Yet attractive, intelligent women just seemed to fall apart when he spoke to them. I shook my head, I never understood it. I wouldn't mind some of it; whatever it was.

Back at the site we mounted the gearbox and lined it up to the pinion. In the days before laser aligning all we had to help us were dial indicators and using them we got the gearbox aligned to within .01 mm, about four one-thousandths of an inch. That was close enough for Jeff.

The last part of the jigsaw was the motor, all two thousand horse power of it. The owners had bought a new motor for the SAG mill which was still a few weeks away, but we fitted the existing motor to the ball mill and again lined it up. We just needed the sparkies to pull their massive cables to the motors once the trenches were dug, and we could check direction before we assembled the couplings.

Electricians earn more than us blokes doing mechanical work for doing infinitely less. Generally they are a strange bunch (must be working in all that ionised air or something). Still, I did feel a twinge of pity for the poor bastards on one particular afternoon when they were suffering out there in 40° heat.

'Want a hand?' asked Gary, who shared my disdain for them.

Rosco, a sparkie from Warwick, looked up from his toil, sweat dripping off the end of his nose. 'Oh yes please,' he said.

So Gary and I put our hands together and applauded them, 'Well done lads.'

I felt no sympathy for them. In a few days they would be in one of the switch rooms where they would spend the remainder of the contract terminating their cables in air-conditioned comfort.

Jeff, meanwhile, having finished overseeing the installation of the mills, was about to go on his way. I was sorry to see him leave. He was a hell of a nice guy, knew just about all there was to know about mechanical installation, and wasn't afraid to pass his knowledge on. At the end of the job Jim asked him if he was going to come back and commission the mills.

'No,' he said, 'I don't think that's necessary. Larry's here and he can handle it.' I almost blushed!

❧

We were staying at the Crown Hotel on Mossman Street in Charters Towers. The pub had stood there since the turn of the century and had probably received a few coats of paint in its time. But everything about the structure was original and the room I had was right underneath the old corrugated iron roof. I had been staying there for a few weeks when one night the sound of rain falling on the roof filtered into my sleep. In a couple of seconds I was wide awake. It was pouring and the noise was almost deafening.

My first thought was to wonder if we would have the day off. Half of me liked the idea while the other half didn't fancy it at all. I lay there in the dark listening to the sound and somehow, despite the noise, managed to drift off again. When my alarm went off at six the rain was still coming down and I wondered what the Brothers Grimm would decide to do. It was Sunday after all, so they might give us the day off anyway. I showered, dressed and joined Gary and Ray at the breakfast table. I asked them if they thought we would be working that day or not, but they had no idea either.

I decided to continue as normal. I went out to my car and was about to head up the road to the site when Jim came by. It was still raining quite heavily, and he simply shook his head indicating that work for the day had been cancelled. Returning to the restaurant I sat down again with Gary and Ray and discussed what the day might have in store. I mentioned I might go to church. They thought I was joking, but I wasn't.

I'm not a religious person, but I have attended a few services over the years and this particular morning was one of those occasions when I thought perhaps I should go more frequently.

I have tried just about every denomination over the years—Muslim mosques, Buddhist temples, Jewish synagogues, Catholic cathedrals—and on that particular morning I attended the Anglican Church on Hodgkinson Street. It was a simple service, nothing to write home about until close to the end. The collection plate was being passed around and I was about to escape before it was passed to me when the priest, more or less anticipating a quick exit by some of us, walked among the congregation.

'If there is anyone among us with special needs who wants to be prayed over, please come forward,' he invited.

With that, a tall dark haired man who had been sitting just ahead of me made his way to the front and stood before the altar. The priest soon joined him and asked,

'Malcolm, what do you want me to pray about for you?'

'Father, I need you to pray for help with my hearing.'

And immediately the priest went into action. He put the finger of one hand in Malcolm's ear, placed his other hand on top of Malcolm's head, then prayed and prayed and prayed. He prayed to the Almighty to help Malcolm with his hearing, while the rest of us in the congregation joined in with great enthusiasm. After a few minutes, the priest removed his hands, stood back and asked, 'How is your hearing now?' Malcolm looked at him and replied, 'I dunno, the hearing ain't 'til next week.'

&

After the mills, we installed a couple of dozen pumps, stripping each one, checking and replacing as necessary the liners and impellors. The pipe fitters ran their pipelines from the pumps to the various destinations, kilometres of carbon steel and stainless steel pipe in various diameters started to arrive and hundreds of new and used valves needed to be checked for operation.

The boilermakers were assembling the tanks starting with the big CIL (carbon-in-leach) tanks where the gold is introduced to the carbon and the science begins. The CIL tanks had been cut in half so that they could be transported, and now had to be welded back together. The plant was really starting to take shape and I was so pleased to be a part of it.

58

The cyclone

Towards the end of the year the plant was almost completed. The powerful motors and pumps had been installed, tanks assembled and tested, motors fitted to the two enormous mills and test-run. The trenches dug for heavy cables to connect to the motors and other electrical equipment around the plant had been filled in and compacted. Mechanical completion wasn't far away.

About a dozen of us were kept on to finish off the place and make sure it was ready for commissioning, after which I was thinking of starting another job with Jeff in the Northern Territory.

But just then the weather changed. The signs had been building up for weeks and we had been working around the clock because the company wanted to get the construction finished before the wet season arrived.

We received a cyclone warning. It looked like the cyclone was heading straight for us once it had crossed the coast. The day before it was due to hit was spent cleaning up the site, making sure anything that might fly was put inside or tied down, and anything loose was picked up and put away.

Jim Paisley drove into the site in his brand new XC Ford ute. He told almost everyone to head back into Charters Towers. (They didn't need to be told twice.) But he asked me, Chris and Russ to stay on site to look after things, and as that meant we'd be paid, we agreed.

It was just after lunch when the skies opened up and the parched ground that hadn't seen so much as a shower in the time I'd been there was soon awash. (The rain in town a couple of Sunday's earlier had hardly disturbed the dust out at Disraeli.) Small streams started to run through, rapidly turning into bigger streams, until the entire site became a lake. It poured with rain for almost two hours, so noisy on the roof that we couldn't hear ourselves talk. Slowly the downpour started to ease until by mid-afternoon it stopped and the sun briefly appeared.

'Come on Larry we'll go and check out the creeks,' Jim suggested.

I looked at him as if he were crazy. 'That's the eye of the storm passing over—there'll be more to come,' I reasoned with him.

'Ah tosh, I've seen heavier storms back home.'

True, if that was a cyclone it was kind of disappointing. I had also experienced worse and for some reason that convinced me to go with him, whereas Russ and Chris, both Australians who had seen what a cyclone was capable of, declined the invitation.

We climbed into Jim's new ute, negotiated the submerged car park and headed back down the road to town. There were three creek crossings, one with a bridge and two others that we used to ford. When we reached the first creek it had completely changed since that morning, with the river quickly turning into a torrent some 15-20 metres across and looking quite deep.

Jim approached the river cautiously—logs were actually floating down it—and as we eased the ute in, the water started to rise until it was half way up the door. Fortunately it rose no further and we made it across.

By the time we'd done the short drive to the second creek it had started to rain again, pouring so hard the wipers couldn't keep up. Then for some reason best known to himself, Jim decided to turn around and head back before we got cut off. He managed a three point turn, retreated to the first creek but drove into it far too quickly. The water ploughed over the bonnet, swamped the engine and we stalled in the middle of the river.

Jim tried desperately to restart the engine but the car refused to fire and the water was getting higher and higher, now almost covering the bonnet. Then slowly, ever so slowly, the car started to move with the current. It was barely noticeable at first, but a few seconds later we slipped off the road and sailed down the creek for a few metres. It was as scary as hell and I wasn't sure what the best course of action was. Opening the door would have taken some Herculean effort and didn't look like a good idea. Jim seemed stunned into inactivity. On balance staying with the car seemed the best thing to do.

The rain fell for the rest of the afternoon as we floated and snagged, floated and snagged, floated into areas where I'm sure they'd never seen an amphibious XC Falcon before. Not that there was anyone around to see us: most sensible people were indoors waiting this thing out.

'Whatever you do don't tell Bill about this.'

'You think I'm going to tell people what has just happened? We've just won the idiot of the year award. No, your secret is safe with me Jim, but it might just come up in conversation when Bill wants to know where the car is.'

Jim looked at me. 'What should I tell him?'

'Oh no. I'll leave that in your capable hands.'

When the rain eased the car was left firmly wedged between a rock and a hard place. Inside the cab was dry, a testimony to the vehicle's sealing qualities, and it seemed a shame to open the doors and flood it, so I opened a window to grab a branch that was hanging over the car. I was able to haul myself out and drop into the creek which came almost up to my waist. Jim followed me, and the two of us started the long walk back to camp.

We had been walking for about an hour and it was getting dark when we heard a vehicle coming. Very soon a truck appeared with Chris and Russ inside.

Jim looked up at them. 'Not a word Russ, don't say a word.' And we drove back to the mine in silence.

The next morning we were up bright and early to recover the ute. Chris drove the front end loader and Jim, Russ and I followed in the truck. The creek was nowhere near as threatening or as dangerous as it had been the previous day and the loader made easy work of pulling the car back onto the road. The whole operation was completed more or less in silence but Chris couldn't help himself.

'Just one question Jim.'

'Go on.'

'Is that what you call Fordin' the river?'

Soon Christmas came around. I phoned home on Christmas Day. It cost me 10 dollars a minute but was worth every penny. Sadly though, Christmas that year stays with me for all the wrong reasons.

Eamon, Chris, Russ, Gary and I were invited to have Christmas dinner with a dozen nurses who were rostered on to work over the holiday period. Unfortunately we'd no sooner arrived at their quarters and had a drink when the ambulances started arriving. Apparently a car going east on the road to Townsville had crashed head on with a car going west and a third vehicle had ploughed into the wreckage. The accident left us feeling numb and useless. One minute the nurses were enjoying the Christmas celebrations, the next they were in casualty up to their elbows. I couldn't do it, but thankfully there are plenty who can.

The next couple of weeks flew by as we had the mills spinning like tops and we started long hours of commissioning the machines and tweaking them to their capacity. I had enjoyed construction, but I was starting to discover that commissioning sucked!

One night in the early hours I got back to the Crown to find a note under the door asking me to call Jeff.

'We start in McArthur River next week. Are you still interested?' he asked when I phoned him the next morning.

'Absolutely. I'll be there in a couple of days.'

In construction you're often hired and fired at five minutes' notice and it works both ways. I drove in to see Jim and Bill.

'I'm off lads. I've got a start with Jeff at McArthur River and he wants me there yesterday. I figure things here are just about finished.'

'Keep in touch.' Jim said offering me his hand.

I went to the workshop, picked up my tool box and said goodbye to the lads. Loyal employees Chris and Russ would stay until the very end while Eamon had been offered full-time employment with the mine.

'You stay out of trouble,' was my parting line to Eamon as we shook hands.

'Why?' he asked, looking more like Steve McQueen than ever.

'Why indeed?' And I was gone.

59

My dad, camping enthusiast

—ഹൈൽ—

I was still in Parkside, so it was probably the spring of 1961. I'm not sure what sparked Dad's interest but he had the idea that he and I should go camping for a week for a bit of long overdue father and son bonding.

'What d'you think son? We'll leave the women at home and head off into the wide blue yonder, just the two of us?'

The women were my mum and my sisters Dene and Debs. I wasn't so sure about the wild blue yonder. I was about 10 and made a noise that 10 year olds make when confronted with an awkward question. My dad obviously took it as OK.

On the Thursday evening I gave him a hand to rotate the tyres on our Ford Popular. It looked like we were off to Scotland or the Lake District, judging by the amount of preparation he was putting in on the car. He started with an oil change, and by the time he'd finished he'd just about given it a full service. He even changed the thermostat, which he told me was the main reason for cars overheating.

While he was doing that I pulled out our tent and the lilos. Mum, being quite resourceful, had made some kind of sleeping bags using a sheet inside a blanket with some plastic stitched to it. Dad was quite enthusiastic about them.

On the Friday evening, after I rolled up the sleeping bags and folded the tent, Dad and I filled the boot of the car. Mum had bought a swag of food. It looked like we were going up the Amazon for a year and by the time we'd finished we were barely able to shut the boot lid.

It was a beautiful summer evening, people were cutting the grass, a game of football was being played on the green, and the neighbours were outside taking in the sunshine. But everyone seemed to stop what they were doing and watched the emotional scenes unfold outside our house as my mum and sister saw us off. There were hugs all round and promises to write often. Although I didn't know where we were going I was certain all would soon be revealed as we reversed into Berwick Road and headed off on our journey.

'So where are we going, Dad?' I asked after we had waved a fond and tearful goodbye.

'I don't know son. Wherever the wind and the road take us,' was his whimsical reply.

The road didn't take us far. To my dad the journey was everything, while arriving was sometimes an anticlimax. For as long as I knew him, the 'brew-up' on the side of the road was one of the highlights of any trip. Unlike my uncles who always favoured the roadside cafes, my dad preferred to stop in a field where he could light a fire, boil some water in a pot and make a cup of tea. This meant something to him, though I never really understood what.

We had been driving for about an hour with the wind and the road taking us east towards the wilds of Essex. I knew we had left the city behind because once we were out of London the buses changed colour. Having turned off the main road, we drove through the lanes at about 30 mph. My dad, in his shirt sleeves with his window wound down and

one hand on the steering wheel, seemed to be looking for
something.

It was a beautiful spring evening as the sun slowly
started to sink behind us, casting long dark shadows across
the lanes and fields. The thick roadside hedges formed almost
a complete canopy above us so that sometimes we were
plunged into darkness, only to emerge from the gloom into
the evening sunshine. It was a perfect English setting.

There was still an hour or so of daylight left when my
dad saw what he was looking for—a place to stop and have
a brew-up. He parked in a clearing, but instead of gathering
firewood he pulled a metal box out of the boot: somehow he
had got hold of a primus stove. He unfolded the box, peeled
the lid back, arranged the legs and the other bits and pieces
before pulling a length of plastic tube from the car.

'I'll show you how to siphon petrol son,' he told me, as
if he was letting me in on some dark family secret.

He removed the petrol cap, pushed the tube into the
fuel tank then sucked until I thought he was going to pass
out. He was almost crossed eyed by the time petrol started to
run into the small container he was holding.

'We don't need much,' he said when he'd taken about
a pint.

After pouring the petrol into the small fuel tank on the
primus he proceeded to pull on a small plunger attached to
the stove. It looked like he was pumping up the primus and
I watched with interest, because I knew this would become
my job soon.

'When you feel a bit of resistance push it back in one
more time and twist the knob clockwise to lock it, OK?'

Yep, I understood.

He then turned on the burner, lit a match and
immediately blew himself to the shithouse!

It all happened in the blink of an eye. One second I was
receiving a science lesson, the next the science teacher was on
fire, or at least his arm was. So was my foot, the grass all

around us, the two plastic sleeping bags seemed to be burning really well, and the rear wheel of the car.

I thought the road was a deserted country lane, so I was more than a little surprised when people arrived from all directions to put us out. The rear tyre, which had been burning fiercely, exploded, adding even more drama to a very eventful evening. It took our rescuers a few minutes to extinguish the half a dozen fires that the primus and my dad had started. Poor old Dad really looked a bit shell shocked, his glasses were hanging on one ear, and he was smouldering!

Our helpers salvaged what they could, changed the rear wheel, dressed our wounds and offered words of comfort—all in a remarkably efficient fashion. It took them just a few minutes, and then they disappeared as quickly as they'd arrived, leaving Dad and I rather scorched and beaten around the edges.

It turned out that they were a coach party on their way to a darts match who, fortunately for us, had just happened to be passing and seen everything.

After a few minutes, Dad started to put stuff back into the car, but not with the same enthusiasm as earlier that day.

'Come on,' he said, eyebrows missing, hair severely singed, glasses broken, 'let's see where the road and the wind take us.'

I was so glad when I realised they were taking us home ....

—⁂—

60

The Northern Territory

I left Charters Towers and had an uneventful run to Cloncurry where I spent my first night. Next day I arrived in the Isa, stopping for a beer in Boyd's because you have to. There were only a few people in the bar when I found the place late morning, so its attraction was lost on me. I'd been told it livened up a bit nearer closing time but by then I was well inside the Northern Territory, land of no speed limits.

I reached Barkley Homestead towards the end of the afternoon. The bloke at the servo there told me the road was open, but that he hadn't seen anyone come down from Borroloola where I was headed since yesterday.

'A few creeks are flooding up there but it's nothing too serious.' he told me. I didn't have a four wheel drive, and so far I hadn't needed one, even though I'd been on some interesting stretches of road. Still I decided to wait until morning to be on the safe side.

Nothing developed during the night, so I set off up 300 k's of dirt road and broke a fan belt half hour into the journey. I then spent an enjoyable hour replacing it with the spare I carried.

This was another wild place, not a soul for miles and the wind in the long grass the only movement. A couple of the creeks were up and running, but they didn't cause me any trouble. I arrived at Heartbreak Hotel in time for a beer and a counter lunch, and then rolled into McArthur River in the early afternoon.

A room had been booked for me. I threw my bag in there and went looking for Jeff. He was on site waiting for me, and later that afternoon we drove up to Borroloola, the port site that fed the McArthur River mine. There on the wharf was the familiar silhouette of another mill shell. Jeff had a look at it, but as it was still in quarantine there wasn't much he could do until it arrived on site.

Unlike Charters Towers there was no real town at McArthur River, just the camp. The Heartbreak Hotel, 10 minutes up the road, was an interesting place on a Saturday night. The guys would come in from the cattle stations to let off a bit of steam and if you wanted a scrap there were always a few who would accommodate you.

One of the ringers used to bring his barber tools in with him and if you bought him a drink you could get a haircut too. The first half a dozen haircuts were usually quite unremarkable, but you could normally tell on Monday morning who'd had a trim closer to closing time.

There were no women apart from a couple of professionals who would come in occasionally from Mt Isa but never stayed, and that more or less describes McArthur River.

The job we were going to do there involved exactly the same procedure as the one we had followed at the Disraeli mine in Charters Towers, and demanded the same accuracy. The weather was always a big factor in that part of the world as during the wet season roads are closed, delaying deliveries and simply delaying work.

We were working with a company out of Melbourne that had won the contract to build a pilot plant. The mine was to produce zinc, lead and silver—very different from our experience of gold production—but that didn't matter, since we were only concerned with crushing and milling at the front end of the process.

The mine, owned by Mt Isa Mines, had initially been called 'Here's Your Chance' when the deposit had been discovered, until someone figured McArthur River had a better handle ....

Steve Bradshaw was the young engineer in charge of the job. He didn't seem old enough, I'm sure he wasn't much older than me, but when you spent some time with him and discussed the process you soon became aware that he knew exactly what he was doing.

Steve and I became pretty good friends. I stand six foot six while he must have been more than a foot shorter, so we must have looked like the quintessential odd couple. He resembled a boy scout in his khaki shirt and matching Bombay bloomers, and taking him into the Heartbreak on a Saturday night was fraught with problems, not least because the randy ringers thought Steve would do if there were no females available. I think I saved his arse on more than one occasion and I don't mean that figuratively.

The job was smaller than the one at Disraeli, the mill was smaller too, but it was interesting work, because putting everything together still required the same diligence and expertise.

Jeff and I ran back and forth a few times to Borroloola and escorted the trucks to the site. Then after the cleaning stage the assembly of the mill had started. I thought my job there would soon be winding up, but Steve asked me if I was interested in staying on as there were still a few miles of piping to be run. I knew Jeff wasn't interested but I had nothing else lined up, so I readily agreed.

The assembly of the mill took us less than six weeks, and now all that was required was power. As usual, the sparkies were running behind, and as there was nothing left for Jeff to do he grew impatient to see his family in Melbourne. I was quite happy when he told me to finish off the job.

I then started running the piping through the plant or 'running spaghetti' as it was called. Although it was a job most pipe fitters don't like doing, I loved it. But jeez it was hot— the hottest place I'd ever worked. I used to carry one of those 'willow' water bottles everywhere as we all did, and I must have drunk gallons of water during the course of the day. February was the worst month. When the generators didn't work, neither did the air-con, which meant we didn't sleep.

One day after we had finished work we came back to camp to find the power was off: the gensets had thrown in the towel again.

'It's over 50°,' the camp manager told us. 'They don't work too well when it gets that hot.'

'Well,' I thought to myself, 'if it's any consolation NEITHER DO I.'

&

When it came to handling liner installation in the new mill we did the job on night shift, as it would have been too hot to do it during the day. Even though a new mill is a doddle compared to liner changes in a mill that is half full of charge, the operation still took us two 12-hour night shifts. I then completed the motor installation and ran up the mill and crusher without problems.

In March the weather wasn't much better, but at least with the power on we had air-con and could get some sleep. By the end of the month the plant was close to completion and I was surprised that I hadn't been laid off, as we were entering the commissioning phase.

Poor old Steve, he seemed to live in the place. I started at five in the morning to get as much done as possible before the sun slowed us down, yet no matter what time I started, Steve always seemed to be there to greet me and he remained after I left.

They were having a lot of trouble with a frothing agent used in flotation, which seemed to be everywhere. Once the froth got into the process water tank the place became one big bubble, and none of the ideas for solving the problem seemed to work. A receiving vessel knocked up by the boilermakers couldn't control the bubbles, and it ended up looking like a giant bong standing in the middle of the plant dripping in slime.

I came in one morning and it was obvious that Steve had been there all night. He was black, and when he removed his glasses he looked like a raccoon.

'It's not working,' he said stating the obvious and finally admitting defeat. 'The board are coming in this morning and they are going to be asking some pretty sharp questions.'

'Like 'What the hell is that?' I offered, pointing to the massive slimy bong.

He nodded. 'What do you think we should do with it?'

'If it was working or at least achieving something you could say it was a prototype, but if it isn't working they are going to question your credibility. Let's pull it down.'

'Yeah, pull it down,' agreed Steve, shaking his head and slurped off for breakfast.

The problem didn't go away, and we later found out the wrong frothing agent had been supplied. Eventually they changed the agent, the bubbles disappeared, and so did I.

Just when I thought I might have a short holiday, I received a message saying the Paisley Brothers wanted me to join them in Pine Creek. I took a quick squiz at the map to see how far away it was, and got ready to leave.

I went to say my goodbyes to Steve to find he was also starting to cross the t's and dot the i's and would be on his way shortly too. I worked with him on a number of jobs over the years until he finally moved to Canada.

The next morning I was on my way again—just a short seven hour trip to another mining town.

61

All that glitters ...

I spent most of that year working in the Northern Territory, in Pine Creek, Mt Bonney, which is neither a mountain nor very bonny. We installed a mill and in a place called Goodhew just off the Sturt Highway south of Darwin.

The Goodhew mill was supposed to be haunted. Apparently a whistling operator had been feeding the thing one day when he slipped, couldn't get off the conveyor in time and fell into the mill. People said you could still hear his ghost whistling. Of course the wind blowing over the bolt holes might have had something to do with it, but it was quite eerie on night shift when you could hear the whistling even when the bolt holes had bolts in them.

After Goodhew my next port of call was the Granites, a gold mine as remote as any place I have ever visited or worked. A dozen of us drove 1500 km to install another pilot plant out in the Tanami Desert, west of Alice Springs.

I decided to continue into Alice for the night. It's an interesting town, but I was growing tired of interesting places and decided that this was going to be my last bush job.

Although the work in the Territory had been good, lucrative and for the greater part enjoyable, as my 25th birthday came and went, I was beginning to feel there was more I should be doing.

The next morning I completed a bit of maintenance to the car and bought another tyre before setting off down the dirt again. I spent the first night under the stars sleeping in the back of the pick-up, something I was becoming more comfortable with, until I woke up shivering with the cold long before the sun came up.

I pulled into a little place in the middle of nowhere not far from our final destination. It was to become our local— a pub, servo and general store called the Rabbit Flats Roadhouse. The owner, Bruce, had a policy that the price of fuel and grog depended on the attitude of the customer which was amusing sometimes when a poor unsuspecting traveller ambled into the shop to pay for his fuel. In those days petrol was about 35 cents a litre but sometimes when reserves were running low in Rabbit Flats it could be as high as two dollars a litre and woe betide you if you wanted to argue.

'Two dollars a litre? Are you crazy?' one traveller demanded to know.

'Two twenty five,' Bruce coldly replied, knowing the next servo was about 600kms in any direction and ready to raise the price again if there were any further objections. The customer always ended up paying and vowing never to return.

A carton of beer could cost anything Bruce felt like charging. He had it, and you wanted it. Whereas a carton of VB would cost about nine dollars in the big cities, we paid 20 dollars, and he liked us!

They had gold out there in the Tanami Desert we knew that. They had us out there after all, and most parts of the pilot plant we had come to install were either there or on their way. However a vital ingredient was missing without which processing gold was impossible.

We needed water, and a drilling crew was searching

everywhere for that precious commodity. Because all the dozens of bores that were sunk came up dry, operations had to be suspended. Bill and Jim had us cleaning the mill and unloading trucks, which I found monotonous, so I was relieved when I was asked to go out and help the drilling crew whose mechanic had to return to Darwin.

I worked with them for a couple of days, long enough to know that working as a drill mechanic is a horrible, thankless, endless job. The drills seemed to have a million moving parts and if the rig was old, as this one obviously was, it was broken down more than it was working. Spare parts were rare and sometimes, if the part you were replacing wasn't exactly a genuine one, you had to be resourceful and make what you could to get the job done.

On my fourth day, when just about everyone had decided that we were never going to find water, a curious and wonderful thing happened. It was mid-morning, still cold, and as the rig was behaving itself for once I was using the time to clean the spark plugs of my car. Suddenly I heard an unusual noise, one that started as a dull rumble but quickly developed into a roar. We had hit water. It blew like a mighty geyser hundreds of metres into the air and then came raining down on us. We danced in the pool that had quickly formed around us, and just as quickly the water soaked back into the arid ground until it wasn't even damp.

We were sitting on the rig feeling quite pleased with ourselves when Tommy spotted some debris that had been blown to the surface. At first glance the stones looked like any others in the area. But then we saw that these stones gleamed, they glittered and they were very heavy. All that glitters might not be gold, but these stones certainly were— we had just drilled through a vein in an alluvial gold field. The three of us rounded up whatever we could, surprised just how heavy a few rocks could be.

We spent the rest of the day drilling but there were no more payouts so we capped all of the bores we had drilled and reported back to camp that we had indeed found a water table. The project was back on track, Tommy and his offsider returned to Darwin, and our secret remained sealed.

With my very heavy shoe box burning a hole and my work almost done I was now looking for the first opportunity to be on my way. I had September 1 pencilled in as my escape day by which time the mill would be finished and the plant 99 per cent complete. Jim and Bill would be laying men off soon and I knew others wanted to stay so I reckoned that my departure would allow someone who wanted to stay an extra pay packet.

That was the last time I worked for the Paisley brothers. I'm not sure what happened to them, but they had a knack of winkling out jobs that no-one else seemed to find. They were a couple of dour Scots who rarely laughed, but while working for them, I had a lot of fun.

62

My dad the football star

—⚜—

Millwall has been my football team since I first saw them play. It was on the opening day of the 1957-58 season when we drew 1-1 with Halifax or Wrexham. My dad's family come from London's docklands and most were dockers, so the Den, Millwall's football ground, was on the doorstep and it was almost inevitable that I'd see my first game there.

I support Millwall because my dad and grandfather supported them—it was almost a tradition. My dad also took me to watch Spurs in the early 1960s when they were possibly the best team in Europe, and I did have a soft spot for West Ham after they won the World Cup in 1966, but as I was a Millwall supporter there was a conflict of interests.

Although I never actually joined a team myself until I was about 12, my dad got me playing football as soon as I could walk. I'm sure he saw a Jimmy Constantine or a budding Duncan Edwards in me.

During the summer holidays, with four or five of my mates, I would go down to the park at the end of our street where the game would start at about ten o'clock in the morning. Slowly more kids would join in until sometimes we'd have two full teams by mid-afternoon. Even if someone else came along after that they were accommodated.

These games would run for hours, the length of the pitch stretching until we ran out of room. There was never any limit to how wide the pitch was either, although we were next to a busy road and after a few close encounters with the 292 bus to Victoria it was decided the road should be a touchline.

We would nip home for dinner, woofing down the meal as quickly as possible. Nothing as trivial as food was going to interfere with our passion.

I played in at least three of those marathons and particularly enjoyed it when the dads came home from work and joined in for 10 or 15 minutes. Some of these blokes had just done a 10-hour day, but they had the same enthusiasm as we did when they saw us. While some were only in their 30s and played well most had more enthusiasm than skill.

It was always a proud moment when your dad scored. I remember playing with my dad once when I was 11 and he would have been 41. He scampered around like a man possessed for 10 minutes; someone passed him the ball, he cut inside and blasted one just inside the near post! I think he retired after that. Magic moment though.

౿

My dad was one of three football dads who taxied us all over London in their cars. Len's dad, Lenny Boy, drove a blue Consul; Rob's dad, Norm, had a big old Zephyr; and my dad was in his Ford Pop.

There were no showers after these games, and our dads must have winced when we climbed in the back of their cars covered in mud, but they never complained and never got a penny's compensation for their trouble. I think they enjoyed it as much as we did.

Les Humphries who was our manager ran an ice cream van in the summer and a paraffin truck in the winter, so depending on the time of year, that is how the rest of the team and most of our supporters travelled to our games. Les also drove a curious felt-covered Jag. There weren't too many kids on a council estate that got chauffeured to a Sunday morning game in a Jag, but it did happen to me on a couple of occasions.

It was a magic part of my life, and the foundation of who I am. The highlight of my career was playing for London Colney at Redbourne Town's ground in the Herts Premier League. It wasn't exactly the top of the pyramid, but I know the crowd paid to get in. My cousin Alan went all the way, playing for Watford and Luton against all the top teams in the country. And it all started in the park at the end of our street ....

—ഇൽ—

63

England beckons

I said my goodbyes the night before, drove into the Rabbit Flats Roadhouse and filled up with fuel. Together with ice and a couple of cartons of VB that little shopping trip cost me over a hundred dollars. I often wondered if Bruce made a huge profit or whether he was just covering costs. Anyway, I was just pleased he was there.

I set off right after breakfast with the sun in my mirror heading for Halls Creek and another 300 kilometres of dirt. Alone on the road again I loved the freedom. Out there it was as wild as ever and I stopped the car every couple of hours and walked around, enjoying the wind on my face.

During one stop I climbed up a hill to look in every direction, almost certain I was alone in this wonderful wilderness and relishing the isolation to a point where I felt a strange pang of resentment if I saw any car approaching.

In September the sun was comfortably warm—without that bite I knew would come in a couple of months. Dressed in just a pair of shorts and thongs, I was still a tender foot but felt I could walk for miles. Back in the comfort and security of the car I pulled out another can of VB from the esky in the front seat. I wouldn't swap what I was doing with anyone, I thought, as I continued on my way.

I pulled into Halls Creek just in time for a counter lunch. I'd grown very partial to Lambs Fry and no one made it better than some of these outback pubs. The Bungle Bungles were close to Halls Creek as was the Wolf Creek Crater, but I was told I'd need a four-wheel drive to get to either location, so eventually decided to continue towards Fitzroy Crossing.

The road, despite being Highway One, the main road around Australia, was not as good as the one I'd just left. I blew another tyre, and as a consequence it took me nearly four hours to travel the 220 kilometres to Fitzroy Crossing.

Whenever I had a breakdown I would try and enjoy it, seeing the stop as an opportunity to rest in a unique part of the world I would probably never see again. After changing the tyre I refuelled in Fitzroy Crossing, picked up some more ice and headed off in the hope of reaching the old pearling town of Broome that night.

I wasn't disappointed. I covered the 400 kilometres in five hours and drove into Broome just as the sun sank into the Indian Ocean. I sat on the bonnet of my car and enjoyed my last beer on Cable Beach. I hadn't seen the ocean since I went for a swim in Fiji a couple of lifetimes ago, so as the sun slipped away I went for a quick dip. My morbid fear of sharks returned immediately however and I soon scarpered back up the beach. I needed a camera to capture all of this I thought. Words are all very well but they say a picture's worth more than a thousand ....

The following day, relaxing in Broome before setting off to Port Hedland, I decided that after three years away from home it was time to go back to England. I hadn't seen the people I loved for too long.

A couple of hours out from Port Hedland I completed my first circumnavigation of Australia. I noticed a point where I had stopped for the night three years before with Adam,

Jimmy, Ivan and Brad, and spent a few minutes there. I toasted them quietly, wondering where they were. Then I was on my way again, arriving in Port Hedland in time for a lunchtime beer in the Hedland Motel.

I phoned Denny, and he and Sheryl joined me for the evening. A foreman now, Denny asked me if I wanted a job. I laughed and politely declined.

But he did get my interest with news of a shutdown they were having in the Tom Price iron ore mine 'just down the road.' It would be an ideal place to top up my account before returning home.

Den gave me a phone number of the contractors involved, so I spoke to them. Then Denny gave them a reference and I had a start. When it comes to finding a job it's always a case of who you know.

The work was only a one week but it would do nicely. I left the next morning, following the railway line into the heart of the Pilbara and through Millstream and Hammersley Gouges into more and more wild, beautiful country.

I arrived in Tom Price, booked into the SMQ and spent five days overhauling more busted pieces of mining equipment. After the job I'd done with Jeff and the Paisley brothers this sort of work was a walk in the park.

The highlight, if that is the right word, came one evening when I was sitting in the public bar of the Tom Price Hotel.

'Who owns the XW ute?' asked a bloke who had just walked in.

'I do,' I told him.

'How much d'you want for it?'

'Three and a half.'

I gave him the keys, he took it for a drive and an hour later he gave me 3,500 dollars in cash. The pick-up had been a good old work horse, never skipped a beat, but it was time to sell and there was no better place to do that than in an outback town like this one.

Two days later, in Perth Airport waiting for my tool box and suitcase, I was back where it all started three years ago. Next stop London.

64

My dad the survivor

—❧☙—

My cousin Alan and I were very close from about the age of 10 to about 15. We played football together, spent our summer holidays together and became like brothers. When our family moved across London to Borehamwood, Alan would take the tube from his home in Kennington to Burnt Oak and get the 292 bus, which would drop him on our doorstep. He did this or I did it in reverse, sometimes not even bothering to tell our parents where we were going. Mothers these days would have seizures if their kids did that, but for Alan and me it was normal.

In 1964, when I was 13, I spent New Year's Eve with Alan in Kennington. We stayed up until midnight emptying all the left-overs from people's glasses into our own. My uncles, when they'd had a few drinks, always dug into their pockets and gave us kids what change they had and my sister Dene and I used to compare our 'presents.' This particular New Year they seemed more generous than normal.

My mum and dad left before midnight. New Year's Day wasn't a public holiday back then and my dad had to work in the morning. They took Dene who was 10 and my four year-old sister Debs with them but I was allowed to stay and enjoy the party.

The next day, after Alan and I gave my Auntie Kit a hand with the cleaning up, we spent the day hanging around the house. I was going to stay for the weekend but then on a whim I decided to go home.

I arrived home at about five o'clock in the evening and as I walked in through the back door, I noticed immediately that something was very wrong. My dad was standing over the stove stabbing the potatoes.

'Where's Mum?' I asked.

'She's gone son.'

'What do you mean, gone?'

'She's left us—she's left home.'

His words washed over me, leaving me in a bit of a daze. I ran upstairs to find Dene sitting on the toilet just weeping.

'What happened?'

Dene was incoherent. She had seen Mum come home, run upstairs and pack a suitcase while her boyfriend sat waiting in his car outside. Dene was too young to understand, but understood enough to know her mum was leaving her. She tried to bar her way to stop her leaving, but Mum pushed her aside and left her crying on the front step. It was Dene who told my dad that his wife had left him.

In those days, in my world, separation and divorce was something that happened only to movie stars and celebrities, not to people on council estates. All my 19 uncles and aunts were married, and out of my extended family and my class full of friends, I was the first person I knew whose parents had separated.

That January was an ugly, horrible month. When Dad tried fruitlessly for a couple of reconciliation meetings, my mother promised to come home and talk over whatever her problem was. I remember leaning out of my bedroom window watching for her car. Every car that turned into our street I wished was hers, but it wasn't. She was supposed to come at seven: at nine I closed the window. Twice she did that.

I didn't realise how hard my mum's leaving had hit my dad. He wasn't an abusive man and there had been no rows or fights—no indication whatsoever that his 17-year marriage was about to come crashing down around his ears. I sat with Dad one Saturday as we were getting ready to go over to my cousin's house. He was tying Deb's shoes when he just started crying. I was useless, never knowing what to do or say. I wish I had.

Winston Churchill died a few weeks later. He was so loved by my dad's family but when my Uncle Harry phoned to talk to Dad about it there were brief words followed by a silence.

'I'm sorry Harry, I've got no tears left,' I heard him say.

I think that was when he hit rock bottom. But it was also a turning point. After that he accepted the hand that life had dealt him and never looked back. He quit a good job to work shifts in a factory so he could be there in the mornings to get Debs off to school. The neighbours were wonderful. Gwen or Mrs O'Keeffe picked Debs up from school and there was always someone waiting for us with a snack when Dene and I came home.

My sister Dene, not even 11 years old, had the lion's share of the household duties dumped on her. She spent Saturdays doing the laundry. She cooked and cleaned and became our surrogate mother while I did whatever I was supposed to do.

But in the end my dad held us together. Although it would have been easy for him to go off the rails he didn't, and I believe we came out of it the better for the experience. I'm always surprised at a man who can't use an iron, or look after himself. My dad showed me how to make the best of a really dire situation. I never did thank him.

I saw my mother briefly in 1967 and again in 1980 but I never spoke to her. Now, years later, I wouldn't know what to say if I did come across her again.

65

Goodbye Oz

L ondon wasn't the next stop. I had arrived back in Perth and booked into the Wentworth Hotel in the centre of town where Lindsay, one of the guys I arrived with as a Ten Pound Pom, got his first job in Australia. The place must have changed hands a few times since then as no-one there knew of him or his whereabouts. Pity, it would have been nice to have caught up with him and compared notes.

I had originally planned to fly home and started making tentative arrangements, but something happened that changed everything. I took a taxi from the airport to the Wentworth which, despite its flash name, was probably the cheapest pub in Perth. There were no porters to hump my toolbox or my suitcase which was just as well as the case finally gave up the ghost on the front step of the hotel.

I'd been reluctant to throw it out because it had been a going away present from my sisters and I considered it lucky, but with my dirty laundry all over the front step I kind of figured I needed a new one before I could board a plane.

It was when I was out shopping that afternoon that

I spotted a back packer and before I knew it the seed was sown for an overland trip back to London. There was an excitement about back packing that jumping on a plane didn't have.

'The adventure continues,' I thought as I looked for a suitable sized pack.

It also became apparent that I'd need to buy a whole heap of clothing and gear for travelling as the contents of my suitcase suddenly looked very dated and useless.

Believe it or not I had stupidly carried a three-piece suit halfway around the world. It was a smashing suit in its day, navy blue with a red chalk stripe that made me look like a British Rail station master. And of course you don't just wear a suit do you? I mean it comes with all the bells and whistles—tie, shoes and shirts. I went through my case and what I found was a museum of the bloke I used to be. By the end of the afternoon I realised I needed none of it and never would again.

These days I wore shorts, thongs and t-shirts. I had a couple of pairs of Levis and a few of the kind of shirts that were as much *de rigueur* in the mid-70s as three piece suits weren't.

I had a carved wooden shark that I bought in Bougainville and a photograph album! But I couldn't bring myself to bin any of it so I boxed most things up and shipped them back to England with my toolbox. Sentimental rubbish. I would open the crate in London in a few months' time and with the exception of the toolbox would wonder why I'd wasted my money.

In my toolbox were the gold rocks I'd picked up at the Granites. I would have tried to cash them in, but one night a bloke in the bar there warned me about the police. The Gold Police or the Gold Stealing Detection Unit was a division of the Perth Constabulary. These thugs were a law unto themselves, the bloke explained, and if you worked in any of the mines in and around Kalgoorlie or tried to cash in any nuggets you could expect a visit from them. I didn't need the money or the agro so I'd left the rocks in my tool box with the idea of cashing them in when I got home.

It took me a couple of days to put together what I needed. I had plans to go trekking in the Himalayas so I bought a really good sleeping bag. I decided I would buy a coat when I needed it rather than traipse one all over Asia. With the good thick jumper that survived my suitcase cull and the same boots that scared the crap out of Leigh's borzois, this was more or less the extent of my luggage. I bought a ticket to Singapore and left Perth with no fanfare whatsoever.

66

Singers and other cities

For me, Singapore was always a city that really wished it was in some other location, preferably Europe. I'd always found it a very sterile, boring, expensive city, and this time nothing had changed. On my first visit I'd been told that I had to visit a number of landmarks, including Bugis Street with its cross-dressing and transgender communities. When I saw women I considered far too gorgeous to ever fancy me, I concluded, with my logic, that these women were obviously men. The first time you see them it is difficult to believe that they are not women, but after a short time the novelty disappears. I went looking for a beer.

A good place *not* to buy a drink, especially when you are on a tight budget, is the Raffles Hotel. You'd need another mortgage if you ever ordered a Singapore Sling, let alone book a room. I had a beer instead on Clark Quay beside the water, making plans to leave sooner rather than later. The best road in Singapore, I decided, was the road leading to Johor Baru, which was where my journey started.

I nipped up to Malacca, a small port on the Indian

Ocean a couple of hours or so north of JB. I'd served some of my apprenticeship with a bloke who'd spent a fair chunk of the war in a ship just off the coast of Malacca. The very colourful picture he painted must have been coloured by the rum ration, I reckoned.

I caught a bus up the Malay Peninsula, stopping where it looked attractive and spending a day or two in Butterworth, Penang and Batu Faringi.

I crossed into Southern Thailand and fell in love with the place. I discovered Phuket long before it became an international tourist attraction. The Vietnam War had just finished and a lot of the hotels that had catered for the GI's R&R were suffering. That meant quality rooms could be picked up for a song while food, drink, drugs and women were all ridiculously cheap too. Why would I ever want to leave? I hired a motor bike and spent a week exploring the island. My rough plan was to be home for Christmas, so a week was all I allowed myself, but I left determined to return.

I bought a bottle of whiskey and 200 cigarettes and embarked on a seven-day tour of Burma. Clearing customs in Rangoon I was instantly met by black marketeers who gave me a couple of gazillion chat (local currency) for my contraband and then I set off to see the country. I was in a loose group of about a dozen. We had obviously all read the same travel guide and as we exchanged our duty free for the local currency as we discussed our plans.

There were two ways to travel to Mandalay, either by road and train, or by boat along the Irrawaddy River. I decided to go by road and train up and boat back. Why? Possibly a young Kiwi lass swayed my decision. Beryl was a lot of fun and the first woman I had been with in what seemed like a couple of centuries. Sex was inventive and at times amusing. I rarely laughed during sex but Beryl changed all that!

We were in a group of six. David from New York, the language student I'd met in Bangkok who spoke possibly a dozen languages, was on his way to Finland to learn some more. Then there was Stephan from Switzerland, Bernadette, from Australia, and Jimmy a Celtic supporter from Glasgow. We travelled by bus the next day to the old capital of Pagan before catching the train on to Mandalay.

I felt very George Orwell-ish. We booked into the Mandalay Hotel, which in its day was the second flashiest pub in Burma after the Savoy in Rangoon. Beryl wanted to have sex in every hotel we stayed in, and who was I to disappoint her, especially when the Mandalay had a massive four-poster bed?

When we weren't wearing out the bed springs we sampled Mandalay's night life. The place had very Dickensian gas lights and stage coaches and the taxis were Austin Sevens. I'm not sure Dickens ever travelled in an Austin Seven, but if he'd been travelling about in Mandalay when we were there, he would have. We never found a night club, but the restaurants were OK and served their slant on whatever we asked for. What amazed me was the low price of everything. No matter how hard we tried, we hardly put a dent in our mountain of chat.

I became a hippy again spending a day of love and peace meditating at a Buddhist Wat in a place called Sigui. We met some locals who spoke excellent English and spent the evening with them discussing politics and all sorts of banned stuff. Why it was banned I'll never know: it just made me thankful that I come from a country that allows and encourages free speech. The next day I enjoyed a slow boat ride down the Irrawaddy.

While discussing the world's problems and putting them right over a few beers with fellow travellers, I realised I didn't tend to see the issues as being as complicated as a lot of them did. Generally I found our discussions amusing, though I remember having to walk away from one heated argument.

'Christ mate, with your attitude you'll end up topping y'self,' I said to one guy as I left the table. I learned a few years later he did exactly that.

There was a lot of lighter stuff too. We often sat outside the hotel while someone strummed a guitar and someone else played a flute, making music that was well worth listening to. After a couple of beers I always thought I might have been a budding Jim Morrison, but no one else did.

On our return to Rangoon the next day, our group descended on the Savoy Hotel. Beryl and I booked into a suite, ordering room service in an attempt to rid ourselves of a couple of thousand chat. But we found it impossible, so ended up giving it away to the travellers who flew in the following morning. Their flight came in from Bangkok while we flew out to Calcutta an hour later.

67

Sugar and spice

We all parted company in Calcutta for it seemed everyone had their own agenda. Beryl wanted to go to Goa, David to Varanasi, I had designs on Sri Lanka and Jim, Bernadette and Stephan decided to make their way to Nepal. We said our goodbyes and I left the following morning. Calcutta had never been on my list of must-see cities and the short time I spent there did nothing to change my mind.

As I made my way down to the station early in the morning, I passed carts laden with the beggars who had died during the night. Outside the station a boy about 10 sat up against the wall, his eyes open but vacant. Life, like most things in India, was pretty cheap.

I caught the train down to Madras. Travelling by train in India is inexpensive. In fact just 10 dollars bought me a first class couchette. On the leisurely run down the east coast, stopping off whenever the mood took me, I found plenty to whet the appetite.

I was the only foreigner in my compartment and

I enjoyed the company of a number of Indian people who worked and lived in the area. One recently-married couple invited me to spend the evening with them in Samilkot, a fairly large town nestled on the shores of the Indian Ocean. Shah, an engineer who worked at the local sugar mill, tried to recruit me. There was a shortage of skilled workers in the area, he told me, so much so that a bloke with my mechanical background could almost name his price.

Shah and his wife Fatima took me out to a restaurant in Samilkot where I was treated to a wonderful Madras curry that was just on my side of hot. It was a lovely evening. The heat and humidity of the day were blown away on the ocean breeze and a couple of glasses of wine made the thought of working at the Samilkot sugar mill seem quite attractive.

The evening passed quickly as we chatted and for the first time the name of the mill owners, Tate & Lyle, was mentioned. I chuckled to think that I had served my apprenticeship just up the road from the Tate and Lyle factory in London's Silvertown. Who'd have thought I might be working for them in India?

I fell asleep to the sound of the surf and the sweet smell of Jasmine. I could get used to this, I thought, as I drifted off. In the morning Shah took me to the sugar mill. I was half sold on the idea of working in such an ideal location. The climate was a touch on the warm side, but no worse than the conditions I had experienced in the Northern Territory, and things might have worked except that the manager turned out to be a mouthy little upstart from West Ham! The alarm bells had started ringing the previous night with the mention of Tate & Lyle, and after five minutes in this man's company the thought of working for him had no appeal at all. I said goodbye to Shah and thanked him for his hospitality. He didn't understand.

'Millwall-West Ham.' I told him. He still didn't understand.

'Is it a tribal thing?' he asked in all innocence.

I laughed. 'Something like that.' It wasn't the first time that football loyalties had come between me and a good job, and it wouldn't be the last.

The rest of the trip down the east coast to Madras was never dull. From the air-conditioned comfort of my railway carriage I saw the Indian landscape run out into the ocean. I never tired of watching the sunrise, or of smelling the sweet fragrance of cherry blossom or jasmine wafting into our compartment. I read, I wrote, and I conversed with the other passengers, all of whom spoke better English than me.

I would get off the train whenever the opportunity arose and bought chai, but I shied clear of the suspicious little packets that smelled gorgeous, but could have proved treacherous little time bombs.

It was when I returned to my compartment after one of these little trips that I first met Christine and Edna from Switzerland. They joined the train in Madurai and we were almost inseparable for the next month. Christine was tall and funny while Edna was shorter, beautiful and funny and for some reason both seemed fascinated with me! I was delighted to find out that they were also heading for Sri Lanka.

They instantly brought a brand new dimension into my life. Until their arrival I had engaged in polite correct conversation with my Indian passengers, but the girls brought out my mischievous side. We enjoyed long amusing and, at times, risqué conversations. Like most Swiss people they spoke half a dozen languages including almost perfect English with just a hint of an accent. They were a lot of fun and as I learned later, totally uninhibited.

Leaving the train at Tuticorin we walked the short distance to the docks in search of a ferry to Colombo. The place was teeming with the kind of people that railway stations and the docks seem to attract. For them these two teachers and a fitter were obviously loaded, and they descended on us. I kept my wallet and passport in a money belt wrapped around my waist and how I never had anything lifted can only be put down to the fact that I had nothing worth lifting.

We found the ferry office but although the port had been open for about a year, there seemed to be no real timetable or schedule. We were simply told when we purchased our tickets that the ferry would leave when it was full. There were a number of tramp steamers that plied their trade crossing the Palk Straight and in hindsight it would have been quicker and cheaper to have taken one of them to Colombo.

The ferry left in the evening and we arrived in Colombo the following afternoon after a crossing of about 20 hours— a hell of a long time for what seemed like a short hop. Christine, Edna and I then had to fight our way through the mass of humanity that seemed to be heading wherever we were going.

We squeezed through customs, joined the crowd going up the hill to the station and booked second class tickets on the evening train to Trincomalee. Arriving there early the next morning, we were just in time to see the sun rising out of the Indian Ocean. What a beautiful morning that was.

The madding crowd appeared to have dissipated on the train journey. We had changed trains up in the hills and gradually there were fewer people. As we stood outside the station at Trincomalee the locals seemed uninterested in us. With fewer beggars around and fewer kids, who always seemed to have a hand in your pocket, I felt comfortable for the first time since leaving India.

Trincomalee is a beautiful, natural, deep water port on the east coast of Sri Lanka and the seed of my interest in coming here was sown during my apprenticeship. One of the tradesmen who trained me, Dennis Lush, had spent four years in the dockyard in Trincomalee, so my tea breaks and lunchtimes were spent listening to his vivid and detailed stories of Ceylon as it then was. Now here I was years later trying to walk in his footsteps.

We found a hotel in the heart of town that reminded

me of the one where I'd stayed in Fiji, an old colonial place with old colonial prices. It had been built before the war and hadn't seen a lick of paint or any improvements since. The big rooms had large verandas opening onto a busy square and huge four poster beds, but the hotel's best feature was its Palm Court where they still served afternoon tea at four o'clock. Edna and Christine may have wondered why a 25 year-old virile male was so eager to scamper back to the hotel for tea but when they tasted the scones, cream and jam for the first time they felt exactly the same.

The three of us not only shared the room: we shared the bed, the bath, the shower—everything. I have never had two girlfriends at the same time. The cost of something shared three ways was cheaper than shared between two so I guess they saw me as a convenience rather than as a boyfriend. But like Beryl the Kiwi they enjoyed sex and were totally uninhibited. We had a lot of fun.

We spent four days in Trinco, where every day was better than the one before. We would get up late before making our way up to Nilaveli Beach to swim, surf or snorkel. We would wander back for afternoon tea and then in the evening we'd find a place to spend a few hours drinking a little too much before returning to the hotel to re-test the bedsprings.

I was just waiting for my bubble to burst but it didn't. On the evening of our fourth night in Trinco, after heading down to the harbour for some people-watching, we met Matt and Pat from California, a couple of thirty-somethings who were sailing around the world. We immediately fell into sync with them and before we knew it were invited aboard their 36 foot sloop.

They had heard of a place called Adam's Bridge, a small island chain between Sri Lanka and India where the diving was supposed to be unbelievable, visibility was forever and ... what the hell are we doing here? Before the evening was over we had arranged to sail with them to Adam's Bridge.

The next morning we booked out of the hotel and while it was still dark, slowly edged the yacht out of its mooring and sailed on the tide. We slipped out of Trincomalee harbour hugging the coast on a North West setting.

As the sun rose over the ocean and I gave Matt a hand to unfurl all of his sail, I felt a wonderful sense of anticipation. I was dressed in a pair of shorts and the ocean and sky were azure blue with specks of white foam dotting the waves.

This was a far cry from the slate grey sky off the Kent coast at home where I had spent a couple of weekends sailing on the Medway wrapped in waterproofs and a heavy coat. The watery sun had made a brief appearance before an afternoon shower had wiped out all visibility and what remained of our enthusiasm. Sailing on the Indian Ocean that morning was so different. It remains one of the highlights of my full life.

Pat and Matt took turns at the wheel while I trimmed and adjusted the sails as instructed. I was a keen apprentice. We went over the horizon, briefly out of sight of land, and I used a sextant to pinpoint our position. Dolphins broke the surface of the water in front of us and raced with us for an hour or so. It was a magic day.

The sun sank behind the island as we continued to sail North West. At about midnight we saw the light that indicated we were just off Point Pedro on the northernmost tip of Sri Lanka. We changed direction, now heading due west until the lights of Jaffna lit up the southern sky. I don't know what time it was when exhaustion finally took over and I went below but I felt cheated. I didn't want the day to end.

We arrived at the marine park in the early afternoon of the next day to see half a dozen boats of various sizes dotted across the straights. I had no idea what type of etiquette was required or used in such situations. As soon as Matt dropped anchor he and Pat put on their scuba gear and over they went. I am the second worst scuba diver in the world but I do enjoy snorkelling, and for the rest of the day we messed about in and on the water.

Later in the day we moved to another location and found the chain of shoals that runs for miles between the tip of India and the northern tip of Sri Lanka. In places the shoals run just below the surface—evidence that once upon a time a bridge between the two countries really did exist. It is a diver's paradise, full of all sorts of marine life, and for the next couple of days we explored various parts of the reef.

On the evening of the third day, however, I sensed that Christine and Edna were not enjoying it as much as the rest of us. There was no friction, but I wanted to leave before any developed, so when we went into the port of Rameswaram the next day to buy supplies we said goodbye to our hosts.

I bumped into Matt and Pat a couple of times more on my travels. I visited them at their home just outside San Diego, and the last time I heard from them was a Christmas email from the Andaman Sea off the coast of Thailand in 2004.

We caught the train, crossing the bridge back to the Indian mainland. Sri Lanka had been a wonderful interlude. Had it only been ten days? As the sun set on that little adventure I wondered what might lie ahead. In our first class compartment from Madurai up to Goa on the West Coast, Christine and Edna had washed and were getting ready for bed. Edna relaxed in the top bunk, topless, brushing her thick dark hair while Christine sat across from me with just a towel wrapped around her painting her nails. I shook my head. Decisions, decisions.

ॐ

We took the train up the West Coast stopping briefly at a couple of places on our way to Goa. I was hoping against hope that Beryl would still be there, and searched frantically in all the usual haunts in a vane bid to get the four of us together. What an event that would have been. It possibly would have killed me but I would have died a happy man. Alas it never happened.

I found Goa to be an expensive, commercialised version of what we had left behind in Sri Lanka and so did my Swiss friends who were getting close to the end of their holiday. Where southern India and Sri Lanka were almost free of tourist and backpackers Goa was full of them.

Almost without warning, Christine and Edna were on their way home. They had been such wonderful company, so amusing, intelligent and enthusiastic for almost anything, that I had to wonder what they found in me. We travelled up to Bombay together and when we arrived they headed out to the airport. I missed them as soon as they were gone. We exchanged addresses, promising to get together when I arrived in Europe, but I never saw them again, and I've often wondered whatever became of them.

I spent a depressing day in a cheap hotel in Bombay before continuing with my adventure. One door closes— another opens, I said to myself as I jumped on a series of trains that led me through central India. I spent forgettable days in Bhopal and Lucknow, before trading trains for buses on my way to Nepal.

68

On top of the world

I crossed the Indian border with Nepal and traded a bus for an interesting truck ride through some of the most beautiful and scary terrain I have ever travelled. I don't know how many gears the driver had, but just when you thought he was about to stall another gear was found and we ground through the foothills of the Himalayas. Wreckage of other vehicles, some of it quite fresh, littered the mountainside so I was more than a little relieved when we finally arrived in Kathmandu.

I really was a hippy now. I had been a token hippy in Melbourne but now I was treading the Hippy Trail. I even looked the part with a kaftan I had bought in India, my shoulder-length hair and a joint behind my ear. Oh yes, if the old man could see me now!

There were a lot of familiar faces from the Burma trip. The danger about this place was never wanting to leave and I found a number of Europeans, mostly French, who had sold their passports, their blood and were now begging on the streets. I have always had a dozen good reasons not to piss on a burning Frenchman, and this lot simply made that list longer.

I enjoyed buffalo steak, found a restaurant that cooked it just the way I liked it, and spent a couple of evenings in there. That was where I met up again with Stephan and Bernadette who I'd travelled with through Burma. They had been up to Pokara which was high above Kathmandu and on the way to Annapurna base camp, one of the destinations I wanted to visit. They told me where to get a trekking permit and the next morning I was in a small party bound for Annapurna.

The bus left at first light to take us as far as Pokara, a town about four hours west of Kathmandu, nestled on the shores of a lake of the same name. As we were walking through Pokara on our way to the start of the trek, I decided that this little location deserved more of my time and I made a promise to myself to spend a day or so here when I returned.

There were five of us in our little group, Tom, a guy in his fifties from Melbourne, Johan from Switzerland who was about my age and Hans and Gunter two Germans in their thirties. The bus had been climbing all the way from Kathmandu and as soon as we left the streets of Pokara we found ourselves walking straight uphill. I had about 15 kilos on my back, not a lot, but after an hour it seemed to weigh a ton. Johan was fit enough to set a brisk pace and I tried to keep up with him, but after an hour I had fallen to the back with Tom who seemed to be pacing himself.

Tom had done a lot of bush walking but nothing like this, he admitted. The rest of the group were spread out, content to follow Johan. I didn't have a lot of energy for small talk which was just as well as onward and upward we went.

We had been warned that we wouldn't make our destination in one day because we hadn't left Pokara until noon, but were told that after about six hours we would come across a cabin where we should stop for the night. As five-thirty approached, Johan slowed down so that we could catch up. We didn't want to lose anyone in the gathering gloom.

We had made just a couple of brief stops of no more than 10 minutes and I thought we should have come across the cabin by now, but nothing was in sight. As a group we hardly knew each other, yet there was a sort of loose camaraderie growing among us and Johan's dropping back strengthened that since he spoke German and acted as a translator between Tom and I and the two Germans. Somewhere along the way we had picked up a couple of Japanese trekkers as well. They spoke no English and simply smiled politely.

Just when we thought that we might be sleeping under the stars and were about to call a halt, we saw a light up ahead. It took us about another 20 minutes to finally reach the cabin, by which time it was totally dark with just the stars and a bit of moonlight to guide us. Stephan opened the door to discover a fire burning in the fireplace and the smell of something cooking.

'Hello, I thought I was going to spend the night on my own,' a familiar voice told us. It was Jimmy Stewart, my Scottish mate from Park Head.

'The people you meet eh?'

I've enjoyed some nights in odd places with strangers but that night was one of the best.

The following morning I said goodbye to Jimmy again as he returned to Pokara, and we continued up the mountain. It took us another five hours of hard climbing to get to Naggakott but it was worth it. What a view we had when we got there—we were on top of the world. I was captured. It was easy to understand people spending years up in these parts.

I found a nice little boarding house on the lake run by a retired Gurkha, and after dropping my pack in my room I went out to enjoy a cold beer in his beer garden overlooking the lake. Who should be sitting under a tree enjoying the afternoon peace? Beryl.

'The people you meet!'

She wasn't alone—people like Beryl rarely were—but she was genuinely over the moon to see me. I enjoyed a week up there catching the sunrise over Everest, rowing on the lake and experimenting with magic mushrooms and hash. The brilliant food included curries, fish out of the lake, buffalo steaks, unusual salads and different desserts. The beers were always cold and the conversations endless.

Sitting around a table in the garden one evening I counted nine different nationalities present. Two guitars, a flute and a harmonica were produced, and we held an impromptu concert. It was a totally different world from mine, and I could have easily stayed, but after six days I had to return to the real world.

69

Back down to earth

A week later I was back down to earth, boarding a crowded bus in Amritsar bound for Lahore in Pakistan. Amritsar is quite a nice place and I'm sure I could have grown to like it but the unrelenting hoards never eased and ruined the place for me. I was travelling with Barbara, a blonde woman from New Zealand who was continually being touched up or spat at—hardly conducive to good karma. I did my best to be an English gentleman, but it seemed like there were thousands pestering her and I was hopelessly outnumbered.

We passed through Lahore, Peshawar and up into the Khyber Pass. (It's a horrible part of the world and they can have it all to themselves.) Then it was on to Afghanistan, where Barbara finally stopped being tormented.

Afghanistan was like a breath of fresh air, a breath of very cold fresh air too. It was mid-November, snowing in Kabul and for the first time in a long while I was shivering. I needed a coat, and what better place to buy an Afghan coat than Afghanistan?

I didn't need much prompting from the group to try to

head to warmer climes. I was now travelling with David the American linguist who I kept bumping into, and it seemed every time I saw him he had acquired more junk. He was collecting clocks and seemed to have hired the services of three attractive young women to help him carry them, Ronny and Karen from Boston Massachusetts and Linda from Preston, UK. (Linda was the one who told me that Jerry Booth from the long running TV soap *Coronation Street* had died!)

We woke up one morning in a frozen room with no plan for the day. Huddled there under my blankets and coat, I suggested we move along to Kandahar, an idea that was quickly given the nod. So we all trooped off to the bus station—me, David, Ronny, Karen, Linda and five clocks.

I don't know what we expected in Kandahar. It was just like Kabul only smaller and colder, but for the first time I felt I was getting closer to home.

I had about five weeks until Christmas, and I wanted to be back a few days earlier. I'd been gone three years and three months, and as much as I had enjoyed backpacking in the sunshine, this part of the trip was losing its appeal.

Next we embarked on a 16-hour bus journey to Herat, probably the lowest point of the entire trip. Arriving at ten in the evening we then had to try to find a hotel, totally weighed down by David's clocks.

'If you can't carry it yourself, you've got too much.' Who said that? I did.

Things were kind of blah for the next couple of days. We travelled up to the border with Iran. I had a visa but it still took me four hours until I was standing on the Iranian side. Wasn't I the lucky traveller? Well it seems I was, as three of our party had some error with their paperwork and weren't admitted. Barbara the Kiwi, who I kept running into, was one of the unchosen ones and had to return to Herat to get another visa.

I was on clock duty with David who was sweating cobs in case all of his carriers didn't get through and he'd have to break in someone else at further expense.

70

Trouble on the border

If things had been dull, bordering on boring, for the last couple of days it was all about to change, and I would have exchanged boring for what was about to happen.

Iran is an interesting country I'm sure. Many people have told me I should have done this, that or some other thing, but I was now just sprinting from one country to another with a clock.

Travelling from Tabriz to Tehran we found one of the few hotels that would take Christians. Needless to say it wasn't the Ritz or anything worth writing home about, so we stayed a day—just long enough to arrange transport out of the place. Then we caught the first available bus to the border.

We missed our connection in Bazargan and the bus we did catch got to the border after it was closed. All that remained in this freezing windswept outpost after the bus had returned to Bazargan was David, Karen, Ronny, Linda, me and six clocks, I'm sure they were breeding.

It was dark and starting to snow and there was nothing in any direction except a small compound, a hundred or so metres away. I went down to the buildings with Ronny in an attempt to see if we might at least be able to rent a room for the night, but all we found were about a dozen or so border guards who were about to have a party. Their eyes lit up when they saw Ronny, and the request for a room was open to negotiation.

Most of the men spoke a little English, enough to understand our situation, and when Karen and Linda turned up, the Iranian lads thought it was Christmas or the Muslim equivalent. Apparently the reason for the party was that one of the guards had just become a father.

Things started innocently enough with a few glasses of wine and a bit of blow. Yes, we were smoking dope with Iranian border guards. Whether this was sensible or not was an open question, but after a few joints no-one cared and the party continued to gain momentum.

The men were dancing with each other which appeared to be standard practice and David, who seemed to speak almost every language under the sun, was engaging a few of them in conversation. I was chatting to Linda while Ronny and Karen were deep in conversation with the rest of the lads. It was when they started dancing with Ronny that things started to go off the tracks. She was a good looking woman about 26 years old, quite well built, and the boys started arguing among themselves about what I'll never know. Arguing became shouting and before we knew it punches were thrown, a pistol was pulled and a shot was fired ....

I'd never been in a room before when a shot was fired. The noise was deafening, and created absolute panic. There was screaming and mayhem as everyone tried to escape through the same door or window.

Ronny, Linda, Karen and I were outside with a couple of the young guards who then led us down a path to another building, showed us in and locked the door. They seemed to have our best interests at heart which I thought was pretty decent of them. As more shouting continued outside, another shot was fired, bringing more yelling people banging on the door. One of the guards with us checked the door, let another two in and quickly locked it again. The four guards were talking excitedly, and I got the impression someone had been shot. David was missing yet no-one seemed too concerned.

Although it had gone quiet outside things were becoming very uncomfortable. We were in the guards' barracks where they slept. I was told I could have a certain bed as the guy who usually slept there was on leave and an uneasy peace descended on the place. But I didn't like it. If they thought I was going to fall asleep when there was a lunatic outside with a gun, this wasn't going to happen.

I could hear Ronny down the other end of the dorm getting pissed off with a guard who was saying something about wanting to be 'like a brother' to her.

'Brothers don't touch their sisters like that where I come from,' I heard Ronny say, which was more or less my cue.

'OK. Leave her alone.' I said, pulling up my jeans. I always believe I have more authority with my pants on.

I walked down to where Ronny was sitting with the guard, surprised just how easily the guy stopped what he was doing when I appeared. Then more agro started. Outside another shot was fired, there was hammering on the door, a window was smashed and someone tried to climb through. This was Keystone Cops stuff. The invader was repelled with a chair, a fight broke out and during the madness I suggested that we slide out through another door.

We raced across the open ground towards the unmanned border post, and I realised we were crossing into no man's land between Iran and Turkey. Suddenly Linda's clock started chiming nine, hardly ideal for a covert invasion of Turkey. Not surprisingly we were shot at again, although this time the firing went over our heads from the Turkish side. There was an abrupt order, we dived into the dirt and the clock continued to sound all nine of its chimes.

The three big bald-headed Turkish border guards who

appeared also thought it was Christmas when they saw three blonde women trying to invade their country. These ugly guys looked like the real thing, right out of the film *Midnight Express.* I'm not sure who was more concerned, the three women or me, but right out of the blue the gunfire was returned, the three Turks quickly retreated to their compound and we returned to Iran just as quickly, clocks and all.

That was enough excitement for one night. We arrived back at the Iranian border post and returned to the compound, where some semblance of peace had been restored. A couple of the younger guards greeted us with apologies and David appeared, quite unaware that we had just done a runner without him. I thought that we might have triggered some kind of international border incident, but the guards just laughed.

'No, we shoot at each other all the time, it breaks the boredom—keeps us amused,' one of them explained through David who was beginning to realise what had just happened.

An ambulance arrived from Bazargan to take the wounded guard away, who had been shot in the thigh and was bleeding quite badly. The Turks were blamed. I was sure a few more questions would be asked in the morning, but eventually everyone found a bed. Even though the women had to sleep with their clothes on I think they were just relieved to have a place to sleep.

Next morning we had breakfast with the guards, and at about eight we crossed the border.

'Oh look,' said Linda as we climbed aboard a bus, 'we were in the middle of a minefield.'

Mount Ararat could be clearly seen on the northern horizon, its peak covered in snow. Noah's Ark is parked up there somewhere, if you believe the stories, and another time I would have gone looking for it, but this was another one of the million things I didn't do during the trip.

71

The Pudding Shop

The bus took us to Erzurum where we took the train on to Ankara. Along the way the girls were perpetually pestered and spat at. It infuriated me so I could imagine how much they must have detested the attention.

We managed to get a compartment but the train guards and conductors insisted in trying to separate us. When we tried to lock the compartment the conductor brought the police down and we were accused of riding without a valid ticket. These hassles continued all the way to Ankara and by the time we arrived there we just wanted to get out of this stupid, backward country.

We saw nothing of the Turkish capital. I'm sure there is a lot to see, but the agro wasn't worth it. We saw the best of the station though and that was watching it disappear behind us as we left for Istanbul.

To be fair the trip from Ankara to Istanbul was uneventful, allowing us to snatch a bit of sleep. We arrived at the ferry at five am, caught the ferry across the Bosporus and reached the European side of Istanbul about an hour later.

A fleet of taxis met the ferry and after about a week of
travelling and living on next to nothing I decided to indulge
myself. I wanted to find a good hotel with hot water and a soft
bed as soon as possible, and I think the girls had a similar thing
in mind. David opposed the idea, saying that we were wasting
our money, and for the first time in the couple of months I'd
known him I let him have a long overdue mouthful.

'I'll do whatever I like and you, sunshine, are more than
welcome to do as you please too.' And I gave him back the
clock I had carried from Delhi, or was it Agra?

An hour later I was in a bath and an hour after that
I was asleep.

The next day was December 1, and I needed to get going
as I had arranged to meet Ronny, Linda and Karen. They too
had decided to spend their money on a decent hotel room,
probably something more expensive than mine. Roughing it
is OK for a few days, but every now and then you need a tub
and a bit of space. Anyway, I was glad to be with them, and
I was surprised how pleased they were to see me. We had lunch
and met with some familiar faces.

'You need to find the Pudding Shop,' Linda told me.
'Apparently a lot of truck drivers go in there who'll give you a
ride to England.' She had already met someone and was
preparing to go.

'Where's the Pudding Shop?' I asked.

'Just ask any taxi driver to take you there.'

So that night Ronny, Karen and I went down to the
hotel lobby and hailed a taxi to the Pudding Shop. We had to
wait to be seated as the place was seething and there seemed
to be plenty of truck drivers. Managing to get a seat by the
door I got talking to a couple of blokes who were English and
were returning to England.

'When are you blokes leaving?' I asked them.

'Tomorrow, probably tomorrow night. We're waiting ...'
the guy was explaining when a group of four Turkish lads
burst through the door. The last one in left it open, letting in

the wind and snow, and when I told him to close the door he hit me! I rocked back, bouncing off the guy behind me, and launched myself at the one who had hit me. The need to have a scrap had been festering in me since Pakistan and now I'd been given good reason.

I thought I might have found a few allies from among the truck drivers, but I was very wrong and the ones I'd been with scarpered. Even the waiters who I hoped might remain neutral teamed up with the four who came through the door, which made things a wee bit one-sided. I did manage to throw one more punch before I was given a bit of a hiding. My Afghan coat was ripped into one long piece, my glasses went west, my false tooth went in a similar direction and I received a cut over my eye. I still had my wallet but I lost my watch and ended up lying in the street in the snow.

When police arrived they brought me into the café where I was handed back my glasses intact plus my dental plate which must have surprised the shit out of someone when it landed. The waiters were all rabbiting a hundred miles an hour to the coppers about how the fight was all my fault.

The police eyed me up and down and when they had heard enough I was whisked away. I was taken to the hospital first and stitched up. I thought I might have been charged for the stitches, but as soon as the nurse had patched me up I was taken to the station and put in a cell. Oh this was going to be a fun night, I could see that.

I've heard enough about Turks to know that they don't mind a bit of ass play, so I spent the night with my back to the wall. It seemed a long night, not unlike a few I have known, with drunks and crack heads brought in at regular intervals. By the time morning came there were 13 of us in that tiny cell. I had no idea what the score was.

I was sitting there feeling sorry for myself when help arrived from an unexpected source. The cage door was opened and a copper gave me the nod. I thought nothing was going to happen while I was sitting there so I left my perch somewhat reluctantly and followed the copper who escorted me to another cell. There, large as life, I found David of the Clocks.

During the night the girls had gone in search of him because they knew he could speak a little Turkish. I didn't imagine that he had any legal skills—he wasn't the sharpest razor ever stropped—but jeez, he was a convincing liar and had an excellent handle on the language. By the time he had finished he obviously convinced all present that there had been a miscarriage of justice. However, I had been accused of smashing up the Pudding Shop single handed, and the people from the Pudding Shop wanted their pound of Pommy flesh.

David convinced them to allow me to leave and bring back my passport on condition that I would have to report to the police station every day until I went to court.

'When am I going to appear in court?' I asked.

'A date hasn't been set,' he told me as we left the police station. We walked up the hill towards the hotel, and as I was feeling about as low as I could when it dawned on me that I wasn't being taken back to the hotel by the police but was out on a kind of honour system.

'David I'm not being escorted.'

'What d'you mean?'

'I mean that the law have absolutely no idea where I am right now.'

'But ....'

He tried to protest. I think he may have come to some agreement with the duty copper. I didn't know and I didn't care.

'I'm out of here Dave.'

I returned to the hotel as quickly as I could to pack and before I knew it I was in a taxi on my way to the truck park. David stayed with me until I got into the taxi trying to convince me that what I was doing was wrong, but I was determined I wasn't going back to the police station. In fact I began to think the police had planned things this way. If I'd been stupid enough to return they'd have processed the arrest but in reality they were more than happy to see the back of me.

Before David could say another word I thanked him for his help, wished him well with his clocks and told the taxi driver to take me to the truck park.

It was late morning when I arrived at Londra Park. The English truck drivers recognised me before I saw them. I was expecting a bit of a mouthful as they approached me, but instead they offered me their sincere apologies.

'You wouldn't believe the agro we get into if we find ourselves in bovver,' was the first explanation.

'They impound our trucks and our loads—the paperwork is endless,' was a quick second.

Seeing me with a shiner and a couple of bruises, they obviously felt that they had let me down. I thought so too, but now I understood. I didn't tell them that the Old Turkish Bill might be looking for me. I just said I had been released and wanted to get away as soon as possible. One of the lads had a room at the Park that he told me to use until they left that night. Another bloke took my thirty three foot Afghan coat and got it sewn together again. These were gestures of remorse that I quite liked!

It was a long day. Every time I heard a siren I thought it was the entire Istanbul police force out looking for me. On one occasion a police car did come in, and did a quick turn of the Park, but he was moving too quickly to be looking.

Eventually at about ten o'clock that night, Dave, the guy I was going to be travelling with, came to collect me.

'Ready?'

'I was born ready,' I told him.

'Yeah I saw that last night.'

We left Istanbul and headed towards the Bulgarian border. I knew I wouldn't really feel happy until we got into Bulgaria. I sat up front with Dave and discovered that like most truck drivers he was a Country and Western nut. Merle Haggard, Johnny Cash, Willie Nelson ... I heard all of them as we travelled the 215 kilometres to the border.

It took about two hours to get to the city of Edirne close to the border. We sped through the town after midnight figuring everyone would be asleep. They were except one copper who scared the crap out of me. He had his siren going and lights flashing and I thought for a few minutes this was going to be my lot.

He spoke no English, but made himself understood. We were speeding. He had young children and speeding lorries could kill his sleeping children. I didn't dare to ask how but we understood that if we pooled all our Turkish lira and US dollars he would let us off with a warning. I had a 10 dollar bill—hardly a king's ransom, but enough to save our bacon. He took it, together with about 100 lira, and told us to continue slowly. For the next ten minutes we did.

Half an hour later we were at the border. It was open and the customs guard, ever vigilant, had to be woken up by Dave. He stamped our passports and whatever Dave put in front of him just to get rid of us. We then passed through no man's land to be stamped into Bulgaria. For the first time in a few days, I was as happy as Larry.

72
The last leg

Dave drove while I slept, an arrangement I liked. He was bringing a Prime Mover truck and trailer back to London from Saudi Arabia. The truck's beautiful sleeper unit at the back of the cab became my home for the few days I was with him. I had my sleeping bag all rolled out with a couple of pillows and the gentle rocking of the truck made retreating up there at the end of the day an enjoyable thing to do.

Dave had taken a number of fire engines to Saudi, travelling in a fleet of five trucks, and we were still in the convoy. I'd met the other drivers during my time at Londra Park, and as we travelled through the Bulgarian countryside they talked to each other on the two way radio to lift the boredom and keep alert.

As well as fire engines, Dave told me he had also taken some legal contraband with him to add to the profit of the trip. He bought about 20 pairs of Levi jeans in London for a tenner each and sold them for as much as £50 a pair in Tehran, Bagdad or, in this instance, Jeddah. With the surplus he then

bought genuine Persian carpets for about £100 a pop and sold
them for twice that amount. All in all his original outlay of
£200 returned about £2000—not a bad mark up for a sideline
and all perfectly legal.

In Bulgaria we headed through Plovdiv before stopping
in Sofia for fuel, a meal, and for Dave to snatch a few hours'
sleep. The next day we entered Yugoslavia, passing through Nis
then on to Belgrade. It was snowing and the entire landscape
looked quite bleak. I stared out of the truck window watching
country after country just whipping by.

I had left Ronny and Karen in Istanbul and because my
getaway had been so quick and dramatic, I hadn't been able
to tell them my plans. I knew Linda was going to be catching
a truck like me, but I thought that the two American girls
intended taking the Orient Express to Venice before flying
home from Rome, so I doubted I'd see them again. Then to
my surprise, I bumped into them at a truck stop just outside
Belgrade.

They were so pleased to see me and we talked non-
stop, David having explained to them about my escape from
the clutches of the law. We were settling in for what could
have become a very amusing afternoon but both of our drivers
had a schedule to meet. The girls were indeed making for
Venice whereas my truck, unfortunately, was heading for Graz
in Austria where the boys in the rest of Dave's convoy were to
pick up a load of timber.

Although I toyed with going to Venice, the weather
was far from ideal for hitch hiking and I had lost some of the
interest in travelling since I left Perth. I made a loose promise
to meet the girls in St Mark's Square in Venice on a certain
date but when we got to Zagreb where our paths separated
and I looked at the frozen people scurrying around in the
arctic conditions, the thought of leaving my cosy cab had
little appeal.

&

We arrived in Graz, just inside the Austrian border, where we eventually found the timber yard the lads were looking for. It was a public holiday, however, and the company supposed to be loading the timber didn't have a fork lift operator. We would have to wait until tomorrow.

'I can't believe it. No-one here can drive a fork lift,' Dave said to the four other drivers in disbelief.

'I can drive a fork lift.' I told them.

'You got a licence?'

'Probably.'

In my wallet, secreted away in one of the forgotten corners, I found my Bougainville licence book carrying the relevant authorisation. I showed it to Dave who in turn showed it to the guy from the company, and before I knew it I was loading timber onto the back of their trucks.

'Be careful, you are not insured,' was the only instruction I was given.

It took about an hour and a half to load and tie down the timber on each truck and at just after three in the afternoon, we were ready to leave. But the manager of the yard asked me if I would load another couple of waiting trucks and offered to pay me cash in hand for the entire day, so I accepted.

I thanked Dave and Mal and the other drivers for their company and watched them drive down the road as I loaded another truck. I ended up working a 10-hour day, and the manager paid me the equivalent of about eight dollars an hour, so I walked out of the gate with 80 bucks in my pocket.

In fact I didn't walk out of the gate at all. The manager gave me a lift to the railway station, and that night I caught the train to Munich.

On arriving in Munich the following morning I found a reasonable hotel, and that evening I went out to the Olympic Stadium to watch Bayern Munich play Eintracht Frankfurt in a UEFA Cup game. The team I went to see was a shadow of the great Bayern Munich side that had won three straight European Cups. I did enjoy watching Franz Beckenbauer and

Gerd Muller play, but not on that night in a cold, half empty stadium. I was disappointed at what I saw, as I think were most of the others fans in the ground.

I stayed in Munich for a couple of days, treading water now I was almost home, but not wanting the journey to end. I went to a couple of beer kellers where I met some Australian tourists, but no familiar faces. Feeling I had seen enough, I returned to the hotel packed my bag and caught the train to Rotterdam.

A couple of lifetimes ago I had holidayed in Spain, where I had met a couple of Dutch Indonesians, Rez and Harris, who lived in Rotterdam. I spent the day with them and their very friendly extended family. Their mother did all my laundry while one of the sisters, a hairdresser, attacked my hair. It had been a couple of years since I had been to the barber, and when she had finished I once again bore a slight resemblance to the photo in my passport.

My adventure was almost over, an enthralling experience that had taught me a lot. I liked me. I liked what I had become. I was in my 26th year and had made something of myself. Tomorrow night I would be home at last, but that evening, sitting with Rez and his family around the dinner table, it became obvious to me that the journey was so much more important than the destination.

On the evening of 21 December, Rez and Harris gave me a lift to the Hook of Holland to catch the ferry to Harwich. It was a cold night, and the wind whipped the snow and sleet across the decks. I hadn't booked a cabin and I spent most of the night in a big armchair in the bar. I tried unsuccessfully to get a bit of sleep, but the crossing was rough—the worst I could remember from past experience. Although I'm fortunate enough not to suffer from sea sickness, I was glad just the same when the ferry finally shuddered to a halt.

I hadn't seen the white cliffs of Dover, as most of the trip took place in darkness, and when the dawn did finally lighten the sky, a low mist blanketed everything. A watery sun made a brief appearance and a light rain welcomed me as we disembarked and made our way to the train station.

'Welcome home Lazza,' the sun seemed to say, mocking me, before it was swallowed by a heavy slate grey clouds. That was the last I saw of it for days.

'Yeah welcome home Lazza,' I said to myself as I wrapped my Afghan coat around me.

I was greeted by a Pakistani immigration officer and thought I was remarkably patient with him as he emptied my backpack and all but strip-searched me. Then I was on the train to Liverpool Street station. With three days to Christmas the festive spirit was almost tangible, and the station was lit up complete with a bloody big Christmas tree, which I thought was brilliant. I joined the crowd and caught the tube to Kings Cross.

An hour later I got off a bus that stopped right outside the Shooting Star, the pub where I had my last drink before leaving for Australia.

With just over half an hour to go before afternoon closing time, I threw my pack over one shoulder and walked into the public bar. There, sitting at the same stool he had been using three years and four months ago, was Micky White, a bloke who had been in my class a few hundred years ago.

He had put his empty glass on the bar, about to order himself another pint, when he turned to check who was coming into the bar, and recognised me immediately.

'Lol,' he smiled, 'I haven't seen you in ages. Where have you been?'

I smiled. 'Buy me a drink Mick and I'll tell you.'

Lightning Source UK Ltd.
Milton Keynes UK
UKOW051941261012

201273UK00009B/3/P

9 780957 132535